LEADING
WITH
GRATITUDE

21ST Century Solutions to
Boost Engagement and Innovation

Star Sargent Dargin

Pleasant Vines Publishing

Pleasant Vines Publishing
ISBN: 978-0-9996972-0-7
First Edition, January 2018
Second Printing, December 2018

Contact:

Star Dargin
Star@StarLeadership.com

Printed in the United States of America

Contents

I am grateful to all those who gave me a chance and let me follow my own path. To my grandmothers, Ganny and GG, who infused me with strength and love. To my mother, who started me on my gratitude path before I even realized it by repeatedly telling me not to speak up unless I had something nice to say. It was not easy and took decades, but I have learned to find the lessons in those not so nice things, as well as how to say those not so nice things in a nice way.

Foreword by Rick Tamlyn

As an international speaker and workshop leader, I'm proud of being the founder and creator of "The Bigger Game," a philosophy and methodology that inspires executives, leaders, and individuals to get out of their comfort zones and create intentional positive change.

For almost a decade, I've known Star Dargin (as a graduate of The Coaches Training Institute and a passionate supporter and frequent participant in The Bigger Game and All Made Up conferences); this book is a manifestation of Star's Bigger Game.

While it's her story, it's not just about her, it's about every person in the business world. Imagine, if every person from janitor to CEO approached their job from gratitude, how much better the world would be. Gratitude and playing a Bigger Game go hand in hand.

I recommend all leaders, and those who want to be leaders in business, read *Leading with Gratitude*. It has the science, the tools, the how to, and the stories that infuse gratitude into you as a leader, your teams, and organizations. We need more cultures of gratitude in the world, now.

Rick Tamlyn
Author, Keynote Speaker, Co-Active Trainer
and Thought Leader in the Inspiration Business
ricktamlyn.com

Foreword by Virginia Greiman

As a researcher and practitioner of the governance and management of megaprojects, I have recognized the need for greater appreciation of the perseverance and innovation that is required of project teams to deliver these mammoth undertakings.

Leading with Gratitude is a great contribution to the field of management generally, and to the management of projects and programs more specifically. This book lays out the case for the role of gratitude in successful leadership. It explains the importance of gratitude across cultures and explains how to conduct a gratitude assessment and build a plan and practice of gratitude for successful business outcomes.

In today's complex globalized society, it is essential that our leaders understand the value of gratitude and how gratitude can be integrated into the business environment to enhance organizational systems, improve performance, and, most importantly, as a tool that can create happiness, trust, and optimism. This is an indispensable book for those seeking to improve their leadership skills and obtain better outcomes in their personal and professional lives.

Virginia A. Greiman
Professor, Boston University
Author of *Megaproject Management, Lessons on Risk and Project Management from the Big Dig*

Preface

My Slow Path to Gratitude

Recently, while jogging, I took a spectacular, airborne, skinned-knees-and-elbows fall. I looked like road kill sprawled out in the middle of the road.

When it happened, I heard a crack. I knew I'd broken my ankle. Minutes later, sitting on the couch still in pain, I started laughing and feeling intense gratitude. Why?

First, I didn't get hit by a car as I was lying in the center of the road. Plus, I could easily call my husband with my cell phone (I was grateful he was home!) and he instantly came and picked me up.

I was also grateful that, although I'd moved to New Hampshire two years before, only a few weeks had passed since I'd finally found a primary care physician.

I was grateful I'd just signed up for a quality health insurance plan that would pay for most of the costs related to this injury, unlike the poor plan I had years ago. A plan that required me to pay more than $30,000 to cover an illness.

I was grateful for the crutches in my basement that my sister had just stored there while she was moving.

Additionally, my birthday was in a few days, so I had just put David Bowie's new CD "Blackstar" in my Amazon queue to purchase. Sadly, Bowie died that day; yet, I lived to have another birthday, and for that I was grateful.

In that moment, with my ankle throbbing, gratitude kept me calm. It allowed both pain and appreciation to exist at the same time. I believe gratitude even helped me heal faster.

After 15 years as a conscious practitioner of gratitude, I've built a strong gratitude muscle. So, though I didn't like the reality of being awkward and moving slower, this situation opened my eyes as to just how much gratitude has seeped into my life. Now, gratitude is my religion.

Yet, as far as I've come, I still have miles to go and lots to learn. With every talk I give and workshop I lead, I understand even more about gratitude than I did before. I am compelled to offer what I've learned to others. I'm also inspired by the few who are truly experts of gratitude.

I want the rest of the world to see what I see, to learn what I've learned from the perspective of gratitude. At the same time, I've also learned to not be overzealous and to allow everyone to get there in their own time.

For instance, sometimes gratitude doesn't take hold until experiencing a significant, life-changing event such as death, disaster, near-disaster, or divorce. (Though, my hope is that you will learn how to experience gratitude without first having to experience a tragedy.) For others, like me, gratitude has a way of sneaking in slowly until it becomes too obvious to ignore.

Admittedly, I am not distinguished with multiple degrees (I do have a bachelor's degree in computer science). However, I do have a unique name given to me at birth—Star—and I have a story to tell.

An ultra-shy girl growing up in the 70s in the lily-white suburbs of Boston, my parents were deep-rooted conservative New Englanders. But what I remember most is my mother saying over and over, "Wear clean underwear and don't say something unless you have something nice to say."

Though I can't verify the underwear thing (though I *always* make sure my underwear is clean), the latter shaped me and my practice of gratitude. My mother, who now has Alzheimer's, is still being nice, for which I am most grateful.

This may seem small, but in old New England culture (think Pilgrims), we are known for being cold and standoffish. We never show emotion, work hard, don't brag, and are always "fine."

Relatives from Leicester, Massachusetts, via the Mayflower. Note that even the children don't smile. A very serious New England bunch.

Fine is a generic catch-all word that is used when there is nothing more to say. In New England-speak, *fine* is not gratitude. It is simply the generic answer for "Move on! Do not say more! Don't think about it! Chin up! Move ahead!" I was staring at 40 before I realized I had been *fine* for too many years.

I had spent my life doing what a good girl does. I went to college, got married, and had kids. I was also well-paid as a director of engineering and had a nice house in a pleasant suburban neighborhood west of Boston.

But my husband was also cheating on me, which I didn't initially realize. Plus, though I had a good career, building it meant that I was often too busy to be an active part of my kids' lives. Things were *not fine!*

Once I realized this, within a short period of time, I started my own business, got divorced, stumbled through the unexpected death of my ex-husband, and raised two boys.

Gratitude became one of hundreds of things that helped me get through it all. It became the medicine I used to learn who I was and consciously create the life I wanted. (Okay, wine and friends were helpful too, but gratitude was, and continues to be, part of my everyday existence.) Though I haven't always been grateful like I am today, looking back, I now have gratitude for a number of the events that have made me the person I've become.

For instance, I am gracious for growing up in a time and place bursting with technology. Our bucolic, suburban neighborhood was just a few miles from the corporate headquarters of the now defunct tech giant, Digital Equipment Corporation. (My mother worked there as a secretary and I was one of the few latch key kids in our neighborhood.)

Because of my exposure to this type of tech, I started doing computer programming in school on a donated PDP-11 computer, beginning my professional career as a software engineer in a research and development group in 1982. I worked on speech technology and touch screens, two pieces of tech way ahead of the rest of the world.

Regardless of the various formal titles and roles I held, I was responsible for observing, finding patterns, connecting others, and bridging (or translating) the complex to the practical. This connector/ bridge type of role has encompassed my whole life and is the basis for my eclectic career both inside and outside corporate walls.

I pride myself on being a lifelong learner who offers a gentle nudge for the brilliant. I've rubbed shoulders, had brief conversations, and feel privileged to know some of the most intelligent folks in the world.

In 1985, for example, I worked on the project team that gave Stevie Wonder a synthesizer with a voice that could talk to him. That same voice later became the one the late Stephen Hawking, a world-renowned physicist, used too.

In another instance, I sat with two colleagues in a meeting room at Microsoft headquarters as its stock went public. You could hear the cheers rumbling throughout.

I've flown to Silicon Valley on corporate jets to meet with leading-edge technologists and I've even sat in meetings with one of the founders of the Internet itself, Vince Cerf, and watched him passionately and elegantly trash a room full of engineers.

(Being a young woman who barely spoke up, a female in a male-dominated field, I spent a majority of my time in the background. Thus, most of these amazing people and companies don't even know I exist.)

Ultimately, I gave up coding after a few years and moved into management, where I fell in love with connecting the dots and aligning vision to reality. I've held several director-level positions at large and small companies, yet, in 2000—after 18 years in the corporate world—I dropped out to launch my own business and achieve that elusive work/life balance.

Today, I get to work with equally brilliant clients in one-on-one coaching sessions and small workshops. It's the same type of work as before, except I don't have to manage anyone! I simply observe them to find patterns, adapting my feedback based on *their* needs so that they can fully lead their teams.

Yes, I still yell at my cat, swear at my husband, and get mad at my grown kids. (I also still utilize my family as a reluctant, yet fertile, petri dish.) When I catch myself in these states, I simply double down on my gratitude practice. The trick is to self-identify when I'm not in balance.

It's been said by those much wiser than me that the best teachers are those for whom the lesson did not come too easily. For me, the lesson came slowly and sometimes painfully, but it also paved the way for developing the tools I use with clients today (like the Three-Step Gratitude Process in chapter 3 and the GLAD Tool in chapter 7, both of which help you understand and unleash the power of gratitude more easily).

Gratitude isn't about always being happy or joyful, rather, it is acknowledging the reality of the world. So, when all else fails, I look up. And when I look up, I know that I am not six feet below the ground. When I look up, I can see the beauty of the world and the wondrous mystery of this beautiful life.

In the Pages Ahead

In the pages ahead, you will learn the tools and techniques necessary to infuse more gratitude into yourself, your team, and your organization. You will also learn how to apply gratitude in the moment using the GLAD model:

G—Gratitude. There are hundreds of research studies on gratitude and more underway, enabling us to now prove its benefits scientifically. Successful leadership models (and the leaders within then) have gratitude at their core, even if it is hidden or has alternative names, like appreciation.

L—Lessons. In the pages ahead, you will meet gratitude experts and learn the lessons they've shared. We will also look at some of the most common, yet difficult business situations and see how gratitude impacts their outcome.

A—Analysis. The third part of the GLAD model involves the analyzation of gratitude through a process similar to what is already used in many organizations today. Analysis encourages the use of data and facts to create a shift to gratitude. It uses processes similar to those commonly used in emotional intelligence work.

D—Doing. This final step involves building a customized gratitude plan and practice for you, your teams, and your organization. A gratitude assessment and inventory are provided to help you measure your gratitude baseline so you know where you begin. From there, you'll learn the steps necessary for developing a plan that will grow gratitude and populate it throughout your organization's culture.

At each stage in the process, I'll share with you my own personal experiences, as well as those that have been shared with me by clients, family, colleagues, and friends. However, the names and details of the circumstances have been changed to protect the anonymity of the individuals and their respective companies.

Additionally, at the end of each chapter are reflections (discussion questions) designed to help you and/or your team reflect on what you already know. The internal reflections ask you to examine your own personal beliefs, opinions, and observations about yourself, whereas the external reflections call on you to examine what you've observed and experienced. Your answers are the starting point to creating your own personalized, custom plan to gratitude.

Gratitude has a way of elevating every area of your life. If used correctly, it can easily become your key to success in business, as even a small investment will bring transformative results. It also makes you feel good physically, like a runner's high, because it fills your brain with dopamine. After a tragedy, gratitude is also a way out of grief, offering you a new way to see the world.

What makes gratitude so powerful is that it puts a spotlight on what we have, not on what is missing or lacking in our lives. It shifts our focus and allows us to move through what are sometimes harsh realities, helping us work towards a more promising outcome.

With gratitude, we are able to get clear on what we can and cannot change. And even if we aren't able to change a situation or person, we *can* change our approach. We can also change how we think about them and the processes we use to interact with them, providing us with better results.

If you are already a grateful person, I hope this book will validate and expand your gratitude practice and bring more joy into your life. If you are a leader, the world is desperate for more who lead from a position of gratitude. The world is desperate for you.

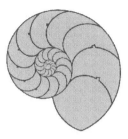

PART 1
G IS FOR GRATITUDE

Gratus, the Latin origin of the word, morphed into *grate* from the mid-sixteenth century, meaning pleasing, agreeable, and thankful. Like *grate* came from *gratus*, the word *great* means *good*, connecting grateful and gratitude to good. Simply put, gratitude is a good thing based on its origin and how we use it.

A versatile word with a long history, gratitude is both a noun ("They operated from a state of gratitude") and an adjective ("I'm grateful for your contributions"). It's also a positive emotion of appreciation or thankfulness ("I'm filled with gratitude").

At its core, gratitude involves not denying or ignoring the hard, difficult, or complex. It also isn't about repaying a debt or feeling obligated or being required to give back, while—at the same time—being more than just the socially acceptable habit of saying "thank you" or being happy all the time.

The definition of gratitude that best serves business (and how it's used in this book) is: "*using conscious appreciation as a way of being; an actionable approach that results in positive engagement and innovation.*"

Hence adding more versatility to the word, gratitude. Gratitude is a skill that can be strengthened like a muscle. As such the stronger the muscle the more benefits reaped.

Most all successful leaders and leadership models have at least some relationship to gratitude. Though, many times, it has either been hidden or is mentioned via alternative names, like appreciation.

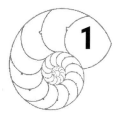

Successful Leaders with Gratitude

You have to serve gratitude in the workplace. You have to express it the majority of the time because that is where you spend most of your time. It just makes sense.

Dr. Mary Falardeau, Owner
Live Free Chiropractor, New Hampshire

Some of the most respected leaders worldwide—whether consciously or unconsciously and regardless of culture or circumstance—have a gratitude practice as their leadership foundation.

That said, how each of these leaders practice and show gratitude varies. For instance, a highly passionate, outspoken, and charismatic leader may heap verbal praise and acknowledgement on employees, while other leaders privately convey their gratitude or never utter a word of appreciation, yet show it in their actions by giving back.

For instance, one well-known media mogul, author, television host, and actress whose net worth in 2016 was an estimated $3.2 billion has been keeping a gratitude journal for decades, and she says it is *the* most important thing she has done. That woman is Oprah.

"I've learned from experience that if you pull the lever of gratitude every day, you'll be amazed at the results," she says, attributing

all of her successes in life and in business to her outlook of gratitude.*
At one point she had even stopped writing in her gratitude journal,
but soon realized that happiness was suddenly missing from her life,
prompting her to pick up this gratitude practice once again.

Oprah believes so much in gratitude that she ends her monthly
magazine with a section called "What I Know for Sure," where she
shares what she is grateful for. She also teaches gratitude to others,
sometimes expressing her appreciation for their talents and dreams
by giving them the financial resources needed to reach their goals
(it's said that she gives away almost $40 million each year).

Her staff gushes over her as their boss. She is caring, acknowledges them as individuals, and creates a collaborative work. Gratitude is fundamental to all that Oprah does. She is a gratitude-based
leader.

Dr. Mary, who provided the quote opening this chapter, also has
a leadership style founded in gratitude. She always has a smile on
her face and projects a level of warmth and optimism that is rare.
Joint owner (with her husband) of a successful chiropractic office in
New Hampshire, Dr. Mary gathers her staff sometimes twice daily
to talk about their challenges and to say what they are grateful for.

The result of Dr. Mary's daily gratitude practice is a dedicated
and loyal staff with no turnover (for which *she* is grateful since she
knows that this isn't the case in similar offices). Her employees feel
heard and appreciated. They do good work and they know it because
she tells them.

Marshall Goldsmith is another successful gratitude-based leader
who works as an executive coach for high-position clients such as the

---

* Note: If you'd like more information on, or wish to verify any of the
data provided in this book, a complete list of resources is provided at the
end.

CEO of Ford and World Bank. After a near-miss airplane incident, Goldsmith consciously embraced gratitude, developing the mantra: "Life is good." He also made his practice of gratitude more public by calling himself a "gratitude radical fundamentalist."

Today, Goldsmith refers to himself as a "philosophical Buddhist," which is more than fitting because Larisa MacFarquhar of The New Yorker previously described this executive coach as "composed of one part Buddhism and one part stubborn Anglo refusal to take misfortune seriously."

In his job, Goldsmith uses what he has learned to tell the most powerful and politically-connected people what they are doing wrong and how to fix it. At least 150 CEOs have hired him to date, grateful for his ability to clue them in on their most ineffective behaviors. Though he deals with difficult and complex issues with these clients, they remain grateful.

Goldsmith is also very open and giving of his time and materials, expressing his gratitude for others by giving back. For instance, his latest gift to the coaching profession was to personally mentor 15 coaches free of charge. The only provision was that those he coached had to also give back to 15 other coaches someday. Over 10,000 individuals applied. Overwhelmed by this response, Goldsmith opened his mentoring program to 100 additional coaches.

A controversial but undeniable successful sports icon who is big on gratitude and beloved by those in New England is Tom Brady, the NFL Patriots' quarterback. Brady is the team's quarterback, a leadership position on a football field.

Outside football, Brady has a reputation for never speaking badly of anyone else and keeping his calm. For example, after losing the 2018 Superbowl to the Philadelphia Eagles, he posted on Facebook, "There are many emotions when you come up short of your goal. And they are all part of learning and growing in this journey of life. Learning turns everything into a positive. And the number one feeling I have had the past 4 days is gratitude."

While he's accumulated multiple awards and records over his long career, Brady has also overcome many challenges. For instance, he faced numerous personal issues, public outcry, and ultimately lost the NFL's support over "deflategate," a scandal for which he was suspended for four games.

Yet, at a leadership conference, I heard Jonathan Kraft, one of the Patriots owners, describe him as a warrior on the field and one of the nicest guys you've ever met. The kind of guy that you wish your daughter would bring home.

Brady and his famous wife Gisele have referenced the book *The Four Agreements* many times. They say it is a key part of their belief system and they reread it frequently. "There is not a wrong word in the book," Brady says.

One of the underlying themes of *The Four Agreements* is gratitude. The author of the book, Don Miguel Ruiz, says: "Why not practice gratitude in every moment until you master gratitude, until it becomes a habit? The more you practice gratitude, the more you see how much there is to be grateful for, and your life becomes an ongoing celebration of joy and happiness."

The practice of gratitude is woven deeply into the fabric of Oprah, Dr. Mary, Marshall Goldsmith, and Tom Brady's leadership behaviors. They all deal with difficult realities, yet they all are also in the top echelons of their fields.

Though the evidence from these leaders is anecdotal, their results and success are irrefutable. Though they didn't all start consciously with gratitude, that is where they all ended up. That makes them great role models to learn from, giving the rest of us a gratitude-based shortcut we can use to hone our own leadership styles, making us more effective to the people we strive to lead.

Realistically, building a strong and deep gratitude practice can help everyone. So why does *Leading with Gratitude* focus on leaders and not managers or individual contributors?

Leaders Make the Greatest Impact

Leaders set a company's culture and tone. Even if the workplace is generally healthy and positive, there is always room for improvement, room for more gratitude, and it takes a diligent leader to keep this front and center.

Additionally, while gratitude is equally effective for all, it is more so for leaders because true leaders deal in change. They create change, acknowledge change, and find ways to make change work. They are essentially the change agents of organizations big and small.

Effectively adapting to these changes is critical to a business's success, both immediately and in the future. So, it only makes sense to start with the individuals responsible for effectuating and monitoring all types of changes within the organization. Individuals who, by creating cultures of gratitude, can make positive changes sustainable.

All leadership models agree that change is a major aspect of leading. A nebulous word, *leadership*, there are hundreds of different types.

Multiple Leadership Models

Having taught leadership for over 15 years, I usually start by asking the question, "How do you define leadership?" I've been given hundreds of different answers and, oftentimes, common themes emerge in the answers, such as those related to the providing of inspiration, hope, vision, and integrity.

Most often though, our personal leadership definitions are based on the people we consider to be leaders. Those we've witnessed in leadership roles either through personal experience or by observation.

For instance, if you've dealt with a leader who is a deeply charismatic charmer, it's likely that, to you, that is what a leader must be. Or maybe you've only been exposed to leaders who are honest and respected, making these two qualities a must in your own definition of leadership.

Or perhaps you have a negative view of leaders and think of them as power-hungry political dictators. In this case, the concept of leadership can be intimidating. Conversely, if gratitude became a word always attached to leadership (which some of the most successful leaders have proven it should be), this term becomes much less threatening and easier to embrace.

Some leaders don't even acknowledge themselves as such. Rather, they feel that they are just responding to the circumstances or changes that need attention or action in that moment. These reluctant or unacknowledged leaders believe they are simply "doing what needs to be done."

In some cases, leadership is forced on individuals by circumstance. During the devastation of 9/11 in New York City, for instance, many "leaders" stepped up and took control of the chaotic and changing situation. In the moment, they dealt with the emergency at hand, undoubtedly saving countless lives in the process.

Regardless of your personal leadership definition, gratitude is a foundational theme available to all leaders. And it can run consciously or unconsciously among them.

To make the matter even more complex, the definition of leadership changes by culture and over time. It changes within industries, within business climates, and within competitive landscape.

Many books and philosophies are available on this topic, each defining leadership as it sees fit. In them, you can learn about the command and control leader, the servant leader, the energy leader, the 21 irrefutable laws of leadership, the emotional intelligent leader, leadership from the inside out, and more!

Despite the differences in definitions and expectations of leaders, gratitude—in one form or another—is one of the foundations in most all leadership styles and models. I literally pulled over 50 books on leadership off my shelves. In all of them, words such as *appreciation, recognition, positivity,* and *thankfulness* appeared. These are all code words used to express gratitude, or are at least closely associated with it.

You might be thinking, "How can it be that all modern leadership models have a gratitude component when there are evil leaders in the world?" The answer? Even evil leaders have been found to have gratitude on some level.

In the textbook, *The Psychology of Gratitude,* authors Robert A. Emmons and Michael. E. McCullough tell us that Hitler, the most iconic evil leader of our day, did express and show gratitude. For example, he was grateful for being born an Aryan (which is cringing to read, I know, and the authors acknowledge this as well).

This type of gratitude is what Emmons and McCullough label as *deviant gratitude,* a gratitude based on ideologies that blind or motivate people, causing them to deviate from a moral compass or social norms. The focus of *this* book is opposite of that. *This* book concentrates solely on developing gratitude as a positive, ethical, and moral foundation to an effective (and good) leadership strategy.

Because there is no one-size-fits-all magic leadership model and each person's leadership style is unique, it is extremely difficult to teach leadership. In fact, I always keep at least 10 leadership models ready in my slide deck, deciding which one(s) to use in a particular session only after learning the audience's management level, industry, and culture.

For example, in general, nonprofit organizations enjoy learning about emotional intelligence, servant leadership, and bottom-up leadership. Manufacturing and the military, on the other hand, are typically more open to disciplined, structured leadership models. Research and development and biotech firms are different yet, as these tend to want more research-based leadership materials, such as those introduced in *Harvard Business Review*.

The irony is that people tasked with developing and researching leadership believe that *their* model is the only one that will transcend industry and culture. Like all leadership junkies, I too believe gratitude as a leadership trait does transcend era, cultures, and industries. But I have also learned that *how* gratitude is implemented varies by leader and culture, and great leaders are always evolving by learning, changing, innovating, and adapting situationally.

Making the decision to become a leader is best done intentionally. That being said, there is no perfect path to leadership, no one way to become a leader, because we all learn differently and at different rates.

It's a process which begins with identifying a leadership model that is closely aligned to where you are now, a model that also includes gratitude as a foundation. Gratitude enables leaders to:

- Handle difficult and complex situations in a positive way
- Radiate calm and confidence to others
- Deal with unknown, changing situations with grace and ease
- Engage, inspire, and motivate team members
- Be creative and innovative
- Quickly accept what is (the good, the bad, *and* the ugly)

A leader's job is to bring a team or company forward, to create a positive work culture, to deliver quality products and/or services, and to make a company profitable—all despite the fear and resistance that can come with these processes and with these changes. When a culture embraces gratitude, change becomes easier.

To show how effective gratitude can be from a leadership perspective, let's take a look at some of the top leadership gurus and see if we can find the connection.

What We Can Learn from Leadership Gurus

John Kotter, Harvard University professor and bestselling author of *Leading Change* and *Our Iceberg is Melting: Changing and Succeeding Under Any Conditions*, says that there are four things that effective leaders do. They:

1. *Motivate and inspire*, energizing people to overcome major political, bureaucratic, and resource-based barriers.
2. *Align people*, communicating via words and deeds with a goal of creating a team that understands and accepts the business's vision and strategies.
3. *Establish direction*, developing a vision of the future and creating strategies for producing the changes needed to achieve that vision.
4. *Promote change*, providing the potential to continue to produce useful changes.

When operating from a place of gratitude, a leader does these things—motivates, inspires, aligns, establishes direction, and promotes change—in a way that makes employees more engaged, thus also providing more positive results.

James M. Kouzes and Barry Z. Posner are two more leadership experts, working together to write *The Leadership Challenge*, a book often considered *the* universal gold standard for developing high-quality leaders. (In an editorial review on Amazon, Marshall Goldsmith calls it the "best research-based book in the field of leadership.")

Admittedly, *The Leadership Challenge* isn't a quick read—it's used as a textbook and the size of a large doorstop—yet, it is filled with measurable, learnable, and teachable leadership behaviors that are not only practical, but used by thousands worldwide.

Kouzes and Posner don't actually come out and use the word "gratitude," rather, it is sprinkled throughout with words like *engaged, celebration, recognition,* and *appreciation.* Positive emotions like these are in the same family as gratitude and the core of their leadership principles and what generates top traits.

For instance, in one part of the book, the authors state, "There are few if any more basic needs than to be noticed, recognized, and appreciated for one's efforts." They also note that companies with a "greater volume of thanks" are the same companies that are highly innovative.

Kouzes and Posner have also been conducting a decades-long study which spans multiple cultures and industries and their data consistently reveals that there are four attributes that over 50 percent of people interviewed want in their leaders to be. Those attributes are:

- *Honest.* We appreciate people who are willing to say where they stand on important principles.

- *Forward Looking.* People want to be engaged in the search for a meaningful future.

- *Competent.* We want leaders with knowledge relative to experience and engaged participation.

- *Inspiring.* Leaders who are optimistic, positive, and upbeat about the future inspire optimal performance.

Using the lens of gratitude, notice how closely gratitude sits underneath all of these. Honesty and competence are two traits proven to build trust, and inspirational and forward-looking are both important aspects of the way Kotter also defines leadership.

Then there's Jack Welch, the CEO of GE from 1981 to 2000. During his time there, Welch increased the company's value by 4,000 percent. Though he was controversial due to his publicized personal scandals and being nicknamed "Neutron Jack" (since he was known for blowing up departments), Welch has become known as an expert in leadership, now consulting and teaching others his principles.

In an article first published on LinkedIn and later by Business Insider, Welch shares, "From our experience, the first essential trait of leadership is positive energy—the capacity to go-go-go with healthy vigor and an upbeat attitude through good times and bad. The second is the ability to energize others, releasing their positive energy, to take any hill." While he doesn't directly call out gratitude, he does mention cousins of gratitude: positive energy and an upbeat attitude.

No conversation on leadership would be complete without the mention of Jim Collins' classic business book, *Good to Great*. In fact, if you've ever heard the phrases "get the right people on the bus" or "confront the brutal facts," then you've already been exposed to the lessons in this book. The companies Collins profiles in *Good to Great* had some of the top financial returns (even higher than GE during Welch's reign), though many were lesser known.

After assessing each one, Collins identified some of the key traits of these top-performing companies. Not surprisingly, there were a few that, in one way or another, related to gratitude. What was interesting, though, is that he also noted what is called the flywheel effect.

If you're unfamiliar, the flywheel is a giant disk that picks up momentum as more people adapt. Like a snowball being rolled down a hill, it turns slowly at first, then quickens (and grows) as it goes.

That isn't to say that gratitude is a magic wand or quick fix, because it isn't. Instead, it is a process, a flywheel, that starts with one person and gains momentum as more and more people practice. It begins with small acts and behaviors that act on each other and start to really stack up, like compound interest.

One of the more personal-based leadership books that had a major impact on me—flipping me from engineer to manager permanently—is Stephen Covey's *The Seven Habits of Highly Successful People*. Named one of *Time* magazine's "25 Most Influential Americans," Covey has become known as one of the world's foremost leadership authorities, organizational experts, and thought leaders. Sadly, he passed away in 2012, but his ideas live on in all of his books.

For instance, in *The Speed of Trust,* Covey used research to show that trust is either built, sustained, or degraded in every transition (again, like the flywheel). He further defines this value on two main dimensions: character and competency. Character trust is built on values a person exhibits, like honesty, whereas competency trust refers to a person's ability to deliver on his or her actions.

Covey goes on to explain that trust in one area does not necessarily translate to trust in another. For instance, it's entirely possible to trust someone personally, yet not trust his or her work. Vice versa, you might trust a person's work, but not trust them as a person.

The faster both types of trust can be built, the more productive a business becomes. This provides a competitive advantage, according to Covey, while also creating a highly engaged culture. A culture that helps people at all levels build positive behaviors supportive of transformation and change.

Trust is also the foundational building block in Patrick Lencioni's New York Times bestselling book, *The Five Dysfunctions of a Team: A*

Leadership Fable. Adapted by 75 of Fortune's 100 top companies, Lencioni's model asserts that, unless there is trust in teams, conflict arises and commitment, accountability, and results are difficult to achieve.

The Five Dysfunctions is a business story that takes a closer look at organizational politics and team failure. Having used tools based on his model myself, I've learned the importance of starting with trust. Results come easier when behaviors are created that acknowledge and show appreciation, appreciation being the definition of gratitude.

Strength-based leadership is yet another popular leadership model and one that relies on an using assessments to identify individuals' strengths. That knowledge is then utilized to place more focus on those strengths versus concentrating on a person's weaker attributes.

The promise of strength-based leadership is enhanced productivity via more engaged employees, thus creating a more positive future. In other words, acknowledging a person's strengths and not focusing on his or her weaknesses goes a long way toward improving engagement and creating a positive work environment.

While gratitude is alluded to in many leadership books and models, it is a ubiquitous word in Brené Brown's work. Though her main focus is vulnerability as those who are vulnerable are what Brown calls "wholehearted people," meaning joyful and happy.

This definition of vulnerability emerged from studying 13,000 pieces of data over 12 years. Brown adds that the definition of leadership intersects with the definition of vulnerability because leadership is the ability to exist in a state of flux, to manage people through uncertainty.

This uncertainty requires the taking of risks and managing exposure, making people feel more vulnerable. "It is asking a lot for people because we are pushing and stretching and doing something that hasn't been done," she says. However, Brown also suggests that successful leaders create a culture where discomfort is normal. With a strong gratitude muscle, vulnerability flourishes. The more grateful, the more vulnerable a leader can be.

Thus, embracing, accepting, and managing vulnerability is what great leaders do. Further, vulnerability can only come from being authentic, which is the birthplace of innovation and creativity. Hence, true leadership comes from authenticity which requires vulnerability. To be more vulnerable, to be a better leader, gratitude must be a daily practice.

Leadership Models	Examples of Models
Change & Vulnerability & Vision	*Rising Strong* – Brene Brown
Motivating & Inspiring & Influence	*What Makes a Leader* – Kotter *Leadership Challege* – Kouzes & Posner
Communication & Culture	*Good to Great* – Jim Collins
Trust	*Speed of Trust* – Covey *The Five Dysfunctions of a Team* – Lecioni
Personal Traits	*Strengths-Based Leadership* – Rath & Conchie *Leadership Challege* – Kouzes & Posner *Emotional Intelligence* – Goleman
Gratitude	*Leading with Gratitude* – Dargin

Why Lead with Gratitude?

Without gratitude, organizations can become filled with unhealthy, thankless, naval-gazing, fear-filled, gossipy, and self-ruminating people. People who are stressed and unable to readily let go of anger, or people who are apathetic, which means their decisions and actions come from a place of fear, if they come at all.

Gratitude is the secret to changing this, one person and one situation at a time. When leading with gratitude, you're able to create a healthy, positive, forward-moving organization. Leading with gratitude changes the focus, changes the problems you have to solve, and it changes their solutions. It also allows innovation and creativity to flourish and can be applied to even the most complex and chaotic situations.

Leading with gratitude creates a connection and appreciation for something outside oneself (it isn't selfish in the least). It's a concept that, in difficult situations, is easy to understand and hard to apply, but tremendously powerful when used. It is amazingly transformational, for individuals and business both.

> Gratitude engages, motivates, and inspires. It creates hope, possibility, collaboration, and inclusion. It is also sustainable. Gratitude changes the problems we solve and actions we take.

Gratitude also does not exist without a comparison. For instance, you may be grateful that you have a wonderful manager because you know based on past experience what horrible bosses are like. Or maybe you're grateful to work for a company that cares for its people because you've worked for one that did not.

Even if you haven't had the experience of a bad boss or have never worked for a company that doesn't value its employees, you likely have heard about or otherwise know of those experiences. This gives you the ability to appreciate what having something means when compared to not having that same benefit.

A statement as simple as "I feel grateful" is still a comparison to a time when you were not feeling grateful. In this way, gratitude is an extremely versatile word.

Gratitude is also an approach or way of being that can be learned and strengthened like a muscle. Though this may sound simple, it isn't always easy. The more knowledge we gain, experiences we have, and older we become, the more comparisons we have and the more we can be grateful for.

Today's organizations face a number of challenges:

- A low percentage of engaged employees
- Changing workforce demographics
- More uncertainty and unknowns
- Shifting and changing industries
- Visibility and instant access
- Demand to stand for more than profit alone

The investment for developing gratitude to help resolve these challenges is low and the risk is low, which means you have nothing to lose by building your gratitude muscle and implementing it as an approach. Gratitude invites inclusiveness in even the most divisive situations.

Leaders live in a transparent world and must assume that they are being watched, recorded, and analyzed at all times. Leading in gratitude supports these more transparent leaders. It is a cure for engagement; connectivity done in gratitude helps prevent polarization.

Takeaways

One characteristic the most successful leaders share is the practice of gratitude. The reasons why they began to infuse gratitude into their daily lives differ, but their continued endorsement of the positive role it plays is unanimous.

While leadership gurus don't call gratitude out as the primary characteristic of great leaders, research clearly shows it as an underlying foundation, often via the mention of gratitude's closest cousins—honesty, trust, authenticity, and optimism.

Embracing gratitude makes you a better leader and brings more harmony and engagement to your team. It also helps you create an organizational culture that is both healthy and positive.

Other key takeaways from this chapter include:

- Using gratitude has the greatest impact for leaders because it helps align everyone with the vision for change.

- Gratitude improves engagement and innovation.

- Gratitude is an underlying foundation on which other leadership skills are built.

- Gratitude is contagious and spreads throughout an organization; it takes only one leader to change the culture.

Internal Reflection and Discussion

1. What is your definition of a leader?

1. Which leadership model do you use and how does gratitude relate to it?
2. How does gratitude relate to your own personal leadership definition or style?

External Reflection and Discussion

1. List three to five leaders you have either known, observed, or read about and describe their key attributes.

2. How do they show gratitude? What actions do they take?

3. What words or phrases do they use that are gratitude-related?

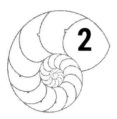

Neuroscience of Gratitude

Intelligence is the ability to adapt to change.

Stephen Hawking

As a single footstep will not make a path on the earth, so a single thought will not make a pathway in the mind. To make a deep physical path, we walk again and again. To make a deep mental path, we must think over and over the kind of thoughts we wish to dominate our lives.

Henry David Thoreau

Brain Science: Facts Not Fluff

The naysayers call gratitude a soft skill (or worse: fluff or woo-woo) because you can't see it or prove that it's valuable. Back in the day, some of us intuitively knew that positive environments and engaged workers offered higher productivity and better results. Social scientists could prove this in a limited way, but typically had to extrapolate the results. Hard sciences like neuroscience can now prove the values and benefits of gratitude.

For example, in his book *Influence*, Robert Cialdini cites a well-known study in which restaurant tips increased by 3 percent when a gift of one candy was left by the waitstaff for the patrons, 14 percent when two candies were left, and, when an authentic compliment was added to the gifts, the average tip increased by 23 percent.

Some waiters already know this intuitively and use it to get larger tips. Yet, the study provided valid proof of this theory as social scientists were able to re-create this effect by conducting experiments that provided the expected outcome.

Admittedly, to translate this particular social experiment into a workplace setting is difficult because of the trouble in defining what constitutes a gift. Additionally, while appreciation shown at work can be equated to compliments, it is unclear whether improved employee productivity equates to "tipping" a manager or employer.

So, what are some scientifically proven ways to create a more gratitude-forward environment at work? One option is mirroring.

Mirroring

Humans are composed of nerves and chemicals that can be measured as they respond to external events. Thus, the study of their emotional and physical states and changes give a broader picture and provide evidence of the benefits of "soft skills," a term commonly used to describe gratitude in business.

A simple example is yawning. We've known for centuries that yawning is contagious in humans, as well as in some animals. Today, using very sophisticated tools to scan the brain, we can prove this scientifically because, if one person yawns authentically (it must be an authentic yawn for this to work), an area of the brain lights up. The same area then lights up in the brain of the person watching, causing them to potentially yawn as well.

Similarly, we copy and emulate other types of behaviors unconsciously. Watch two people talking in an intense conversation and you may see them mirroring each other's hand gestures. Or walk into a meeting where everyone is very somber and serious and immediately you can feel the emotions in the room.

For those working in emergency situations, mirroring is a known training technique. For instance, being calm not only enables emergency personnel to better focus and figure out their next move, it also keeps everyone else at the scene calm. The opposite is true too. If one person panics, others are likely to panic as well.

There are two important concepts here that relate to gratitude. One is that emotions are contagious and gratitude is an emotion we can prove is contagious by watching brain areas light up. The other important point is, like with the yawn, fake gratitude is *not* contagious.

At the foundation of this science are electrically and chemically excitable neurons, some of which have Wi-Fi-like capabilities. This means that they communicate through the air without you having to physically touch another person to pass on information.

The mirror neuron is one example. When seeing someone experience a strong emotion, the mirror neuron unconsciously passes that information from them and you. (It's scary to think that most of the neuron "Wi-Fi" network is unconscious.) Knowing this, you're better able to put this phenomenon to good use.

For example, when people want to end a conversation, they turn slightly sideways, nod, and make a concluding statement. This signals that the conversation is now over.

Some people aren't good at reading these cues because they've not been socialized with them or it may not be part of their culture. Thus, they have to learn these signals on their own. Others are more attuned to what their neural networks are saying, or perhaps because it has always been their cultural norm.

Either way, we can increase our ability to hear these neurons. When you are actively listening to your own neurons, for instance, you are self-aware (mind-body connection). And when you are listening to others' neurons (this involves reading body language), you respond in culturally, sociality acceptable way which is often described as having empathy.

It's important to understand that, like the unseen signals between wireless devices, not all of the neural networks can be heard. Common sayings like, "I had a gut feeling," "I was going to jump out of my skin," and "I felt tingles in my arms" hint at this invisible connection, though today we know that neurons and their networks are behind them.

The expanding knowledge and implications are far reaching and the field of neuroplasticity—a branch of neuroscience—proves scientifically that the brain can be intentionally rewired. This is how we change, and it's also how leaders are made.

Rewiring the Brain

The old adage of "use it or lose it" applies here. In other words, if we don't keep using a particular neural pathway, it becomes weaker. It is still there, but well hidden.

Yet, like a plastic bag, the brain is pliable. This makes it possible to remove old, unused neural networks and create newer, higher performing pathways. (The quote by Henry David Thoreau at the start of this chapter says this perfectly, and, yet, he said it years before neuroscience existed.)

It's like speaking up in meetings. For someone who shares his or her thoughts, ideas, and opinions frequently in this type of environment, talking in front of others is easy. For those who tend to just sit quietly and listen, on the other hand, it is harder to initiate and form ideas on the fly in this particular business setting. Therefore, they're more likely to hold back out of fear of saying something stupid.

Even though the latter person is quieter, that doesn't mean that they've forgotten when and how to speak up altogether. Instead, the adage of "practice makes perfect" applies in that, the more someone speaks out, the better and more comfortable this action becomes.

Neuroplasticity is scientifically backed by the idea that change in the form of rewiring our brain—our neural networks—works. By changing our behaviors, changing our thoughts, and changing our physical body, we can rewire our brain to become more gratitude based.

You'll learn how to do this using a three-step shift in chapter 4. When applied in an organization, one can shift to a culture of gratitude and rely on the authentic, contagious aspect of gratitude to aid in its spread.

Getting Out of Survival Mode

So far, we have shown that gratitude can be learned via practice and that it is contagious. The next important point to validate scientifically is the benefit of working from an approach of gratitude when compared to an approach that is not gratitude-based.

Imagine you are sitting in a meeting and a senior executive starts belittling and disrespecting you and your team for no apparent reason. Unconsciously, your instincts often call upon you to fight back, yell at him or her, deny or discredit the accusations, get defensive, or—in the rare case—throw a punch.

My instinct used to be to freeze, say nothing, and wait until it was over. Other people simply take flight, leaving the meeting or, sometimes, even the job.

Fight, flight, or freeze. We've heard these words before. These are the three reactions our brain instructs us to take when it unconsciously determines we are being threatened.

In the case of an executive screaming at us (or even just thinking they are), our brain acknowledges this as a threat and activates our survival mode. Chemicals and electrical signals are released and passed through our body's well-trodden, neuron survival network.

Because the body is wired to take all threats seriously, when our brain goes into survival mode, we are put in a type of lockdown that won't let anything else happen until the threat is gone. We can, however, rewire our brains to override this survival mode.

To do this requires that we first acknowledge that what each person's brain determines to be a threat is unique. Sometimes they are unconscious and it's difficult to discover the trigger. Other times they are obvious things, like being yelled at.

So, in order to rewire *your* brain and change, the first step is to recognize when you are operating from a survival mode. The second is to find what will shift you out of this mode and into one of gratitude.

For instance, I learned to not freeze when an executive would yell at me. I was motivated because I knew that if I did not deal with this type of scenario, I would be forever stalled in my career.

Initially, I changed my self-talk to ask the question, "What is the worst that could happen if I say or do that?" Today, when I recognize my brain in survival mode, my internal self-talk question has become, "What am I grateful for in this situation?"

It took one executive I worked with a number of months to figure out why he resisted building an open and trusting relationship with a peer who was critical to his success. He knew he was going into survival mode with this person, but didn't know why.

After much self-examination, he determined that it was the other person's voice and vocal mannerisms that reminded him of his ex-wife, with whom he was not on great terms. Just hearing her speak unconsciously sent him into survival mode. Once he realized this, he used logic to override the trigger and went on to have a strong, professional relationship with his peer.

When in the lockdown of survival mode, all of the choices and options that exist revolve around removing the threat. If a person is fearful of losing his or her job, for example, the resulting behaviors and actions will be survival based: leave the job, fight to prove your value and worth, or feel hopeless and stuck and do nothing until leaving becomes the only option.

People who are not in survival mode may take similar actions, but they do them with a much different approach and attitude. They look for creative solutions, take risks they might not have taken before, or use the opportunity to learn and build relationships.

How do we shift out of survival mode and manage the chemical and electric state of our brain, giving us better control over it? Let's try a little exercise.

Imagine a hockey puck traveling 100 miles per hour and it is coming directly at your head from only 50 feet away. What would you do? Most people go into survival mode and rely on their neural network to unconsciously physically move their body, enabling them to cover their eyes and/or duck.

My son became a hockey goalie at age six because, on his team, this position was where all the action was. (He was born with DNA that likes to be in adrenalin-filled situations.) Like many young athletes, my son was motivated to play hockey professionally. He enjoyed studying and researching National Hockey League (NHL) goalies, so I gave him a book, *The Inner Game of Tennis*.

Written by Timothy W. Gallwey, *The Inner Game of Tennis* is essentially a program designed to rewire neural networks, enabling the reader to conquer his or her inner self-critic, self-doubts, nervousness, and lapses of concentration—all of which can keep a player from winning.

This is even more important for those playing goalie as, after watching other goalies over the years, my son learned that this is a particularly vulnerable position. (Mom translation: every time a puck gets by the goalie or the team loses, the goalie gets blamed.) As such, it is also a position where it is easy to self-criticize and not feel supported by others.

The one interesting fact my son learned is that NHL goalies do not blink. They keep their eyes open whenever the puck is nearby, and especially when it is coming directly at them. Not only did this motivate him to avoid going into the survival mode of flight, he also rewired his unconscious instincts to not blink when a puck was coming at him. How did he do it?

My son used self-talk and practiced a lot; I'm talking years. It's also known that, being the younger brother, he was perfect for the goalie role. He was always asking people to shoot on him and, finally, his senior year, he achieved his goal. He didn't blink and had a great last season before hanging up his goalie skates and heading off to college.

My son learned to rewire his brain so that a hockey puck coming at him at lightning fast speeds was not a life-or-death situation; therefore, he did not blink. He used logic instead because he knew that his goalie mask would protect him and he would not get hurt. He was motivated to do this rewiring by his dream of being in the NHL.

While survival mode is good in some regards because it can keep you safe, one of its downsides is that it limits your options. In lockdown, the brain has one goal and one goal only: remove the threat. It can't think of anything else. Thus, practicing gratitude and creating positive workplaces are physically impossible from survival mode, and brain scans confirm it.

The neocortex is where positive emotions like gratitude, happiness, trust, and joy live. Creativity, innovation, and strategy live there too. The neocortex is also where strategic decisions, building and sustaining trusted relationships, and positively handling conflict and difficult conversations are all possible.

Unlike survival mode—which is reactive, not proactive—the neocortex asks questions like: how do I avoid freezing up and, instead, respond to someone screaming at me? Or, how do I make the best of a job and career in an environment that does not work for me? (Rather than, how do I survive this moment?)

Essentially, this portion of the brain can think strategically and ask and answer questions that have long-term implications, while survival mode is limited to short-term. Another aspect of neuroscience that helps us better understand gratitude is the fact that we're biologically wired to work in groups.

Wired to Work in Groups

When you practice gratefulness,
there is a sense of respect towards others.

Dalai Lama

Science tells us that humans are biologically wired to connect to each other as part of survival tactics. In other words, when we are together as a group, we have a better chance of survival since ten people can outwit or outrun a wooly mammoth or build a shelter easier than one.

Granted, the need for outrunning any type of prehistoric predator, a wooly mammoth or otherwise, is gone; however, the biological need to connect to other humans remains. This is even more pronounced in a workplace setting because business today requires us to work together in groups and teams to produce.

According to the U.S. Small Business Administration, one of the main complaints of the 21 million solo entrepreneurs in this country is isolation and its resulting loneliness. Additionally, the most successful individuals in this group have people helping them with business-related needs such as content editing, website-related work, accounting, and social media. In short: achieving bigger results requires working with other people.

All of Tim Ferriss's books, including his most well-known, *The 4-Hour Workweek,* are based on the notion of outsourcing and working with others to get the help you need to become a success. In his compilation book of successful people, *The Tools of Titans,* for instance, Tim shares the brilliance of people who are thriving in the areas of health, living, and business.

In essence, an idea only requires one person to think it and costs nothing but his or her time. But Gratitude provides leverage to this idea and attracts partners who can help support and develop it into reality. In this way, it is the delivering of quality products and services that requires more than one person to achieve.

For instance, in the twelfth century, one person in Italy—Da Vinci— had an idea that man could fly. But one person cannot build a jet in his or her lifetime. In fact, estimates reveal that building a Gulfstream G650 flagship business jet actually requires the help of 1,750 people. Yes, the idea came from one person, but it actually required thousands of people to make.

Since both our biology and our business culture require us to connect with others, why not choose to make these connections positive? Gratitude is a path to creating these positive connections, which are also connections that support engagement and innovation.

In a *Harvard Business Review* article titled, "Why Appreciation Matters So Much," author Tony Schwartz shares a study conducted by researcher Marcial Losada which found "among high-performing teams, the expression of positive feedback outweighs that of negative feedback by a ratio of 5.6 to 1. By contrast, low-performing teams have a ratio of .36 to 1."

What does this mean in real-life terms? Put simply, high-performing teams speak and acknowledge each other in a positive way 60 percent more often than poor-performing teams. How's that for a good outcome?

Connecting Through Gratitude

Imagine a worldwide gratitude epidemic where the more we give, the more we get back, and the more we give again. Gratitude has been scientifically proven to contagiously increase positive behaviors that have real value and real benefits. In the long term, this creates sustainable positive cultures.

The way it does this is by gratitude creating stronger feelings of self-worth, which motivates us to engage in positive social behaviors. When we are grateful, we feel connected and socially valued. When we feel worthy, valued, and connected to ourselves, our team, and/or our organization, we are engaged. This makes us more productive and motivated.

When we feel positive and secure in ourselves and in our place in a team or community, we are more open to alternative opinions and more accepting of people who are different. We become inclusive rather than exclusive and segregated.

In the MIT News article, "Putting Heads Together," researcher Timothy Malone talks about a joint study from MIT, Carnegie Mellon University, and Union College, and concludes that "having a bunch of smart people in a group doesn't necessarily make the group smart."

Instead, to tap into the group's collective intelligence, it must have the right kind of internal dynamics to perform well on a wide range of assignments. These dynamics were defined broadly as social sensitivity, referring to how well group members perceive each other's emotions. (As a side note, the same study also showed that women in general are better at social sensitivity.)

Being attentive to other's emotions can't happen when we are in survival mode since having empathy requires also having appreciation, gratitude, respect, or trust with others on our teams. Gratitude is a basic underlying skill that leads to empathy and caring (social sensitivity) because it is harder to exclude others if you have empathy for them, and you are more likely to listen and respect someone you care about.

Sally Kohn delivered a humorous TED talk in 2013 called "Let's Try Emotional Correctness" that describes this phenomenon. In it, Kohn calls herself one of the most hated people as she regularly receives over 200 hate emails a week. Why?

Kohn was a commentator on Fox News, a media source known for its conservativism. But she is also a progressive and a lesbian. Daily, Kohn would interview and talk with people who had opposite viewpoints, yet her compassion for each person enabled her to build on common ground.

"Emotionally correct" is the phrase she uses instead of social sensitivity and, according to Kohn, people cannot truly listen to each other's views unless they have emotional correctness first. This comes from caring about the other person and gratitude is an external emotion based in caring.

Kohn says she imagines how fearful someone might be of an issue and its impact, making it easier to respond and connect and build trust. Yes, she could respond with hurtful comebacks, but that does not create real change. "Emotional correctness, not political correctness, is how to start the conversations that create change," she says. Gratitude supports compassion and connecting to each other, rather than fighting or hate.

In survival mode, humans connect to survive, to find shelter, to find food, and to defend themselves. In business, we connect to produce profit, for the betterment of society, and to create services and/or products.

Choosing How

Like the jet mentioned earlier, building something this complex requires thousands of people with a shared vision of the completed project. All of their work must be aligned towards the same outcome. One variable that impacts this ability is employee engagement.

Gallup has been tracking employee engagement since 2000 and, after collecting data from 195,600 employees and analyzing 31 million responses, what is known is that roughly 70 percent of employees in the U.S. are not engaged at work.

Additionally, there are 12 measurable attributes that constitute poor engagement. Among them are higher rates of absenteeism and accidents, lower levels of productivity and sales, and a lack of quality of product and services offered.

Done right, gratitude directly impacts productivity in a positive way and results in engaged employees. How? An appreciated employee is an engaged employee, and gratitude is appreciation.

When in an environment of gratitude, positive results happen in less time and at a lower expense. The quality is higher too because the work is being completed by employees who are physically and mentally healthier.

We can choose how we behave when we are with our coworkers and colleagues. We have some control over how we align and structure our work, the culture we create, and the way in which we make decisions and take actions. We *can* choose gratitude.

If you've had the experience of working in a positive workplace, you have likely already seen the tangible results and know that this is more productive. On the flip side, if you've only experienced negative workplaces, you may have an immediate response of, "Yes, that sounds great, but I can't change a whole workplace by just me, one person, being grateful." While it is true that we can only change ourselves, once we do, this changes how other people react to us.

Studies also show that, in the United States, about 60 percent of people are grateful in their personal lives, but very few bring that same way of existing into their work life. Attitudes of gratitude are typically left at the workplace door, even though choosing to bring gratitude into a work setting can expand its impact because it is contagious. Gratitude starts inside us and radiates out, like Jim Collins' flywheel effect described earlier

Collins' research also shows that concepts introduced slowly into the workplace are more sustainable. The more people work together in gratitude, the more positive and productive the work environment becomes.

When we can see how we fit, how what we do aligns to a vision as part of a team or business, we can accept and balance individual and group contributions and roles. Gratitude shows us ways to both influence and be influenced from a connected place of being an individual who is also part of a group.

Takeaways

Gratitude is a practice that can be learned and used in business. Like yawning, it is contagious. Like a flywheel, once it starts and begins to strengthen, it slowly takes on a life of its own and creates even more.

Gratitude can be used by businesses as an approach to constant learning and improvement, which turns into actionable steps for a more productive and positive workplace. It is not an all-or-nothing approach, but rather an inclusive approach.

The more gratitude is practiced and used, the more contagious it becomes and the more it seeps into the culture. Gratitude is an actionable way for individuals, leaders, and business to start positive changes.

Other takeaways from this chapter include:

- Neuroscience has proven that gratitude is not fluff. Science has caught up to what some of us intuitively knew about workplace benefits of happiness, positivity, and gratitude. Some of these benefits are physical, others are social or emotional.

- People can rewire their brains to become more gratitude-based and organizations can shift to a culture of gratitude, using the power of authentic contagiousness to aid in its spread.

- Gratitude takes us out of a counterproductive survival mode and creates an environment for a calm and logical response.

- Humans are biologically wired to connect and work together. Choosing to connect in gratitude creates positive, productive workplaces that are more engaged and innovative.

Internal Reflection and Discussion

1. What triggers you and puts you in lockdown, in survival mode? What will bring you out of survival mode? (For me, it is the powerful question, "What am I grateful for right now in this situation?")

2. For 10 minutes, mirror someone with whom you're engaged in conversation. What happens to them and to you? How can you use this to infuse them with gratitude?

3. What motivates you to want to change, to rewire your brain? After you understand the answer to this question, here's a simple experiment to start the rewiring process: start with something simple like ending your emails in "Thank you" or by removing or changing a negative word or phrase you typically say (for instance, by replacing "never" with "many times.")

External Reflection and Discussion

1. How can you tell if someone is operating out of the lockdown, survival part of the brain? What signs exist? (expressions, gestures, voice tone)

2. Give some examples of people unconsciously mirroring each other.

3. Describe high-performing teams you have been on and how people on them connect and show appreciation for each other.

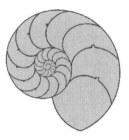

PART 2
L IS FOR LESSONS

Who are the experts in gratitude and how can we learn from them? How did gratitude appear in their lives? Were they born grateful, raised to be grateful, or did some life event spark their gratitude?

Learning to shift to gratitude can take seconds or it can take decades. Understanding the Three-Step Gratitude Process can expedite this shift. Action taken from gratitude leads to better outcomes.

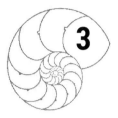

L—Lessons Lead to Innovation

Being grateful in business is just common sense. It's natural to feel gratitude for my employees, clients, colleagues, and suppliers since each is critical for my company's success.

Susan O'Neil
Search Marketing Author and Consultant
Founder of Website Publicity

Despite knowing that his manager fully supported him and gave him excellent raises and promotions, Paul despised the person in charge over him. (In full transparency, Paul is not his real name—or any one person, for that matter—as some variation of this story plays out hundreds of time a day, and in every type of business.)

Paul's dislike came from his manager's poor behaviors, some of which included belittling, name-calling, and never sharing words of appreciation for Paul or his team. It was a difficult and seemingly unchangeable situation.

After three years of trying different approaches with no real improvements, Paul left the company, causing it to lose one of its best and brightest employees. Yet, it was only after becoming grateful for his old manager that it became obvious to Paul how his appreciative behaviors and respect for others were key traits of his own leadership style.

Even though it took him years to be grateful for the gift of clarity of his own style, once he had that clarity, Paul found simple and authentic ways to actively increase his own appreciation behaviors for his team and company. He also learned how to deal with strong personalities, like those of his former manager, that did not have the same style as him.

It was then that Paul's career finally began to soar. This was thanks, at least in part, to his use of the Three-Step Gratitude Process.

An Example of the Three-Step Gratitude Process

Paul's story highlights the Three-Step Gratitude Process perfectly, which consists of:

1. *External—Some type of external event triggers an internal reaction.* In this example, it was the manager who triggered a strong negative emotion in Paul.

2. *Internal—The resulting strong, negative emotion is acknowledged and internal work takes place.* Paul acknowledges his dislike of his manager's behaviors. He was angry and felt disrespected so, after three years of trying many tactics, his response was to leave the company. Years later, when Paul did the internal work and applied the lens of gratitude, he saw things differently. He saw himself as someone who reacted negatively to a manager with a style not like his.

3. *External—An internal shift to gratitude changes the external action.* After doing the internal work, Paul's external actions became different because the problem he had to solve was different. Specifically, instead of deciding to leave a work situation and a manager with bad behaviors, he recognized that he could have stayed and continued to build his management practices while

learning to work with different (even negative) management styles.

While in the course of writing this book, I received an unforeseen phone call from an account representative who manages my relationship with a large, world-leading organization that I've been delivering trainings to for four years. She told me both nicely and professionally that I was being removed from this prestigious account.

For me, "removed" meant not only losing income, but also no longer being able to do work that I love with a client I treasure. My first reaction to this external trigger—the phone call—was physical. Adrenaline pumped through my body and I jumped up and started pacing.

I spent the next 30 seconds in my head, imagining myself in a full-blown screaming tirade aimed smack at her. First, I *attacked*. "How could she do this to me? Next, I became *defensive*. "Hasn't she seen my top-scoring feedback and reviews?" Then I transitioned into *belittling*. "She is the fourth representative for that account and doesn't understand." Finally, I turned to *blaming*. "It will fall apart and be all her fault."

While this account rep was talking, all of these thoughts flashed through my brain, which also meant that I wasn't listening to her. I took a deep breath in an effort to calm down and bring me to a place of being mindful, but this alone was not enough, so I shifted to ask myself this question: "What am I grateful for about this account and this person?"

This was the internal work (step two) and my answer was easy. I was grateful that I was able to impact and engage with brilliant participants and know that I have helped them. I took a few deep breaths, my body relaxed, and I thought of the wonderful relationships and experiences I'd had with the client.

This process enabled me to go back into the phone conversation with the account rep. From a place of gratitude, I was able to calmly ask: "Help me to understand. What is the thinking behind this decision? What recourse do I have to change the decision?" Step three is the external action of asking these questions in this new and different way.

After a few weeks of negotiation with the rep and her manager, I understood the reasons behind her initial action. I also received valuable feedback. My overwhelmingly positive training evaluations notwithstanding, I learned that my perseverance in seeking quality technical support could have been pursued in a way that wasn't quite so abrasive. I could have also shown more tolerance and patience, two areas for me to work on and something I would not have realized without her feedback.

In the end, I was able to maintain the relationship with my client, and, since then, the account rep has also asked me to deliver trainings to two more clients. All of this became possible because, within 30 seconds, I shifted from common behaviors like blaming, attacking, and being defensive, to actually being grateful. The resulted in keeping a prestigious client and getting even more business, instead of severing a relationship and losing precious income.

The Shift to Gratitude

Though the shift to gratitude in my example took about half a minute, it took the previous 15 years of practicing gratitude to enable such a quick response. For Paul, it took three years to figure out what he was grateful for with his situation.

Regardless of the time, the shift to gratitude always, whether consciously or unconsciously, follows the same process: (1) an external situation or event triggers a strong emotion, (2) an internal acknowledgement and reflection occurs, shifting to a lens of gratitude, and (3) an external action is taken.

In gratitude, Paul's choice was to modify his management style and learn to deal with strong personalities who are not like him. In gratitude, my choice was to ask questions to gain a better understanding.

John shared with me that his situation started in 1991, when he was operations manager for a large independent oil and gas exploration and production company in Indonesia. The president of that company was a micro-manager to the Nth degree, constantly stepping in the middle of John's department's business and mandating operating initiatives which often ran counter to its general plan of operations.

While his ideas sometimes had merit, the president would typically impose them without considering the context of the department's day-to-day business. As operations manager, John worked hard to get the operating departments in his area working together and focused on common objectives. The president's mandates often disrupted this effort.

This became more and more irritating, so John wrote a letter to the president, pointing out very explicitly the error of his ways. Before the letter, they bumped heads quite often over management style. After the letter, the relationship became more and more strained.

This tension finally culminated in the company's president maneuvering through the Indonesian work permit system to replace John, and there was little he could do to combat this move. Feeling cheated and disrespected, John stewed over this for years. He felt terrible about the whole thing.

Fast forward to 2009 and 2010, and John was now Chief Pilot for a regional air freight company in Manchester, New Hampshire.

Again, he found himself dealing with an overbearing company president with whom he often disagreed about management style.

As this relationship became more charged, John examined the big picture and decided it was time to walk away from a battle he knew he would not win. He discussed this with the president and, together, they created and executed his exit plan. In this case, they parted friends even though they had very different ideas about how to lead an operation.

A year after the exit, John called the second president and thanked him for the opportunity to work with him. Because he chose to leave in a partnership with the president, with whom he took collaborative actions, John left feeling grateful, energized, and generally happy.

Both work situations ended similarly—John was out. However, in the latter scenario, he left feeling fulfilled, grateful, and ready to move on to the next phase in his life. Or, as John says, they were "very similar circumstances, with totally different outcomes as to the health of my psyche."

Our challenge as individuals (and businesses) is to see how fast we can shift to gratitude--30 seconds, 3 years, or 20 years?

If Paul could have applied the gratitude lens to himself faster than three years, would he have still left? It's hard to say, but by staying and applying gratitude, Paul could have accepted his manager for who he was and learned to deal with the different management styles.

In my story, if I had not shifted to gratitude, I would have permanently damaged the relationship I had with my client, losing them and future clients too. In John's second story, after performing self-examination and adapting a gratitude mindset, he still made the same choice to leave, but those results 20 years later were very different than the ones before he used gratitude.

The faster the lens of gratitude can be applied, the sooner the problems will be different. The faster the lens of gratitude can be applied, the healthier and more innovative the outcomes. The faster gratitude is in the forefront, the more options and possibilities appear.

Gratitude is a steady underlying state, an approach to apply and to shift to when a trigger occurs. If Paul had been able to jump more quickly into a gratitude approach, the problems he needed to solve would have become different.

His questions would have been: "How can I work with this person who doesn't share my leadership style of showing appreciation? Can I sustain the gratitude mindset with my manager's constant bad behaviors? Would I be able to change the workplace culture to one of more gratitude?"

For my story, had I stayed in the negative place of blaming, defensiveness, and attack, the problems I would have been solving would have been: "How do I prove her wrong? How do I discredit her decision? Who is on my side and supports me?"

Bam! or Creeping Slowly?

Pollyanna is a fictional heroine of a 1913 bestselling novel written by Eleanor Potter and her outlook of gratitude changed those around her. It took her a long time working against their resistance, but using consistent, positive behaviors, eventually the town became a friendly and welcoming place.

In the story, when Pollyanna's father died, she had to go live with her mean and wealthy aunt in a cold, unfriendly town in New Hampshire. Her father's influence was strong; he had taught her from a very young age to be grateful playing "the glad game." This game focused on always looking for the positive in everything.

No matter what the reality or how dire the circumstances, Pollyanna could always find something to be grateful for. Yet, her gratitude was tested when she was hit by a car and could no longer walk. Eventually, the gratitude she had previously given to the town and the results of her gratitude practice took hold. The enabled her to shift back to gratitude and walk again.

How a person comes to a conscious gratitude practice varies. Some are raised in a family, culture, or religion that creates the stage for a gratitude practice, while others have absolutely no background in gratitude. Still others have life-altering experiences that bring gratitude into their life instantaneously.

Regardless of which scenario applies to you, a deliberate practice of gratitude can be started slowly or it can occur in a moment—bam! It's your choice! This book and its tools will allow you to decide how quickly or slowly you want to incorporate gratitude in your life.

For me, gratitude crept slowly in. It was there all along, but I didn't consciously create a practice for it until my life reached a low point. Since then, and for over 15 years now, I have been consciously engaged in an ever-evolving practice of gratitude, a background practice that now comes to the forefront more quickly and more frequently when a difficult situation triggers a reaction in me. And I'm not the only one.

Slow, Maturing Process

Mike Foley, a big guy and ex-football player who is in his fifties and always happy, says that, for him, gratitude was also a slow maturing process. Though, it was a worthwhile one as, a now entrepreneur and part-time butcher, he loves life and no longer dreads Monday mornings.

Since his football days, Mike has had a dynamic and, at times, wildly successful career in the corporate world as an account rep. He describes himself as having the "gift of gab" and is action-oriented. In his corporate career, he says that several times he went unexpectedly from what he calls "living the life of Riley," meaning being wealthy and living large, to being unemployed.

Eventually, when he realized that he was sick of people at the top making decisions that effected his life, Mike dropped out of the corporate world completely. For instance, he recalls, one time, a boss telling him to get used to eating hamburger instead of steak, all while bragging about his brand new 40-foot sailboat. Mike needed to take control and ownership of his destiny and no longer wanted to worry about someone else calling the shots.

Each time a major setback occurred--like the loss of a job that would've supported his family for years--the cycle of anger and regret lessened once he was able to let go of the fear and focus on the positive and what he was grateful for. His motto, which he uses in his personal and professional life today, is: "Enjoy today because yesterday is gone and tomorrow is not promised. And always look for the silver lining."

Finding Gratitude Through Adversity

For Marshall Goldsmith, a conscious gratitude practice started after a near plane crash. He was on a plane, it took a dip, and the pilot announced, "The landing gear isn't working, so we need to circle around the airport until the plane runs out of fuel, a necessary step before executing a landing without the wheels down."

Understandably, Marshall was scared for his life, but he also had plenty of time to think. He asked himself what he regretted. His answer? Not thanking enough people who helped him.

Once the plane landed safely, Marshall immediately wrote thank-you letters to 50 people. That's when he became a "connoisseur of gratitude, a virtuoso at thanking" and now regards gratitude as an asset, and its absence a major interpersonal flaw.

For Sheryl Sandburg, COO of Facebook and bestselling author of *Lean In: Women, Work, and the Will to Lead*, it was the tragic death of her husband that started her practice and public acknowledgement of gratitude. In her commencement speech to the class of 2016 at University of California, Berkley, Sandburg said:

It is the greatest irony of my life that losing my husband helped me find deeper gratitude — gratitude for the kindness of my friends, the love of my family, the laughter of my children. My hope for you is that you can find that gratitude — not just on the good days, like today, but on the hard ones, when you will really need it.

Sandburg also said this about gratitude:

People who take the time to list things they are grateful for are happier and healthier. It turns out that counting your blessings can actually increase your blessings. My New Year's resolution this year is to write down three moments of joy before I go to bed each night. This simple practice has changed my life. Because no matter what happens each day, I go to sleep thinking of something cheerful. Try it. Start tonight when you have so many fun moments to list.

The Influence of Religion and Moral Belief

Warren Buffet, founder of Berkshire Hathaway, is one of the world's top ranked billionaires, and he has frequently expressed his gratitude for having been born at the time and place he was, as well as for the wealth he has been able to create.

Buffet shows his gratitude for this accumulated wealth by giving it back to society. For instance, he once gave a $37 billion gift to the Bill and Melinda Gates Foundation. With Buffet's gift, the Foundation reported that it would be able to express gratitude to others on a scale and scope far greater than would have been possible without it.

In 1987, I was sitting in a conference room in Redmond, Washington with my manager and a peer. We were there to discuss modifications to a Microsoft computer operating system and, during our discussions, our hosts left abruptly, after which we heard loud cheering from the company's employees that reverberated throughout the building.

Microsoft stock had just gone public on the New York Stock Exchange, creating 4 billionaires and 12,000 millionaires at that moment in time. (I didn't buy any stock myself because I didn't like how the company did business back then; it was difficult and not responsive. I never would've predicted that Bill Gates would become one of the world's largest philanthropists, doing so much good in the world.)

Research on Gates shows him to be very competitive, hence, Microsoft was also very competitive. This created many legal and ethical issues for the company early on, some related to the early release of poor quality software and being ruthless with partners.

From what I've both read and heard, Gates's religious grounding, his constant reading and learning, and his life experiences led to his maturing over the years, such that gratitude and giving became stronger than his competitive nature.

In a March 27, 2014, interview with *Rolling Stone,* he said:

The moral systems of religion, I think, are super important. We have raised our kids in a religious way; they have gone to the Catholic church that Melinda goes to and I participate in. I've been very lucky, and therefore I owe it to try and reduce the inequity in the world. And that's kind of a religious belief. I mean, it is at least a moral belief.

Both Mike Foley and Bill Gates's paths to gratitude were a slow maturing over time, as opposed to Sheryl Sandburg and Marshall Goldsmith, whose paths to consciously practicing gratitude were a result of a life-changing incident.

When it comes to showing this newfound gratitude in business, there are sometimes barriers as research shows that, while we as a nation can be very grateful personally, we tend to keep it at bay in our professional lives. Why?

Unfortunately, expressing gratitude is sometimes seen as a sign of weakness or a more female quality. Plus, many of us tend to compartmentalize and separate work from our personal lives, thus preventing gratitude from becoming the norm or regular part of our business cultures.

Regardless of how deeply grateful a person you are, there is always more room to bring this quality into our businesses. It may feel uncomfortable and there may be resistance at first, but making this process a success starts with you as an individual and expands to the creation of sustainable business behaviors and practices.

Gratitude Experts

The more you know, the more you know you don't know.

Aristotle

Picture yourself exuding calmness and confidence, regardless of how chaotic, overwhelmed, stressful, or fearful your situation might be. Envision yourself being approachable and giving off a vibe of peacefulness, even while tackling the most difficult business situations (and people).

Who do you know like this? Who do you know who is always calm and centered, exuding peace? The people interviewed for this book are gratitude experts who have a regular practice to support and reinforce this gratitude consistently over time.

Experts Are Always Practicing

Terri Hamilton teaches mindfulness to children and adults. The morning we met, she peacefully and calmly told me how, just prior to our meeting, her computer had stopped working, her printer wouldn't print out a report she needed, she forgot something, and there was traffic on her drive to our meeting.

While all minor challenges, they were all somewhat frustrating. Yet, Terri handled her reality by acknowledging her feelings. She smiled and told me, "I had a lot of opportunities to practice mindfulness this morning."

Terri acknowledges that she is not in a state of mindfulness or gratitude 100 percent of the time, but she does practice it a lot. This enables her to switch to gratitude more easily, and one way to do this yourself is to use the self-distancing technique.

Self-Distancing Technique for Switching to Gratitude

At 14 years old, Malala Yousafzai—the youngest person ever to receive a Nobel Peace Prize—had a man point a gun at her head and shoot her. On October 18, 2013, Jon Stewart of the *Daily Show* interviewed Yousafzai and asked her what she was thinking at the time. Her response:

I started thinking about that, and I used to think that the Talib would come, and he would just kill me. But then I said," If he

comes, what would you do Malala?" Then I would reply to my-
self, "Malala, just take a shoe and hit him."

But then I said, "If you hit a Talib with your shoe, then there
would be no difference between you and the Talib. You must not
treat others with cruelty and that much harshly, you must fight
others but through peace and through dialogue and through edu-
cation."

Then I said, "I will tell him how important education is and that
I even want education for your children as well." And I will tell
him, "That's what I want to tell you, now do what you want."

The first time I watched her interview, I noticed that Yousafzai exudes a calmness and peacefulness that I find contagious. Just watching her, I feel better, even while simultaneously cringing at the horror of her experience. I call Yousafzai an expert of gratitude because, even in a very difficult moment, she switched to positive action.

The unconscious technique she used in that instance is called *self-distancing*. She talks about herself in the third person (instead of saying "I," she calls herself Malala) as a way to separate the strong emotions she is experiencing and allow herself to examine her situation. This technique is a short-circuit out of survival mode and allows you to not fight back, but rather, to choose an alternative. In Yousafzai's case, she chose peace.

Rarely are work situations life threatening. But when you're under stress, the faster you can begin working from a place of gratitude. the calmer you and those around you become. As a result, better and more productive choices appear.

No matter how strong the emotions or how dire the circumstance, being grateful requires us to notice when we are getting in our own way, and to reflect and shift to gratitude. Feeling gratitude for all the things, people, and places in our lives while in the midst of a crisis helps.

Takeaways

Reading the stories of how others have discovered, practiced, and experienced gratitude can motivate and inspire you. It can also provide you with valuable insights into your own experiences.

Here are some of the key lessons of those experts' experiences.

- Regardless of the time it takes, the shift to gratitude follows the same process: an external situation or event triggers a strong emotion, an internal acknowledgement and reflection shifts to using the lens of gratitude, and an external action is taken.

- There is no one way that all people use to come to a practice of gratitude. It can be foundational in a family upbringing, cultural, or religious-based, or it can occur under dire circumstances or gradually over time.

- Gratitude experts are in a state of gratitude more often and can quickly shift into a calm place of being regardless of circumstance. It is a lifelong practice and learning.

Internal Reflection and Discussion

1. What in your upbringing supported (or did not support) gratitude?

2. Was there ever a time or event in your personal or work life that made you feel more grateful?

3. Role play a difficult situation using the self-distancing technique. Does anything shift?

External Reflection and Discussion

1. Compare Paul and John's story. How might the outcomes have changed if their shift to gratitude had been instantaneous?

2. Who do you know (or know of) that you would consider a gratitude expert? Why do you consider them an expert? What are their practices and what impact do they have?

3. What are some examples from society, or a religion, that are about gratitude (other than Thanksgiving)?

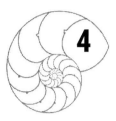

Making a Fast Shift to Gratitude

Any intelligent fool can make things bigger and more complex.... It takes a touch of genius—and a lot of courage to move in the opposite direction.

E. F. Schumacher

Gratitude is like a muscle. The more you build and strengthen it, the stronger it becomes. This allows you to shift to gratitude faster and more consciously, rather than waste energy and time on unnecessarily staying in fear, hurt, and anger—emotions that can lead to ineffective behaviors such as blaming, belittling, gossiping, and defensiveness.

In his 2008 book, *Outliers,* Malcolm Gladwell shares that 10,000 hours of practice are necessary for becoming an expert (a master at something). Though critics say that practicing 10,000 by itself does not make an expert. This practice must also be deliberate.

Deliberate practice is focused and changes as needed. Deliberate practice also pushes your skillset to a higher level. It requires learning and adapting to better match your natural strengths and challenges.

Journaling your gratitude daily, writing letters to those you appreciate, and giving thanks before a meal are all examples of things you can do to regularly practice gratitude. Being mentored by a gratitude expert can also provide you with feedback you can use to accelerate your own skills.

How long you practice, your natural gratitude abilities, and getting expert input to adjust and personalize feedback all impact how quickly you can make a gratitude shift. Bottom line: targeted daily practice is essential.

The Three-Step Shift to Gratitude

The Three-Step Gratitude Process is based on the science of neuroplasticity and is modeled after the emotional intelligence process, which is best highlighted in the Pixar/Disney film, Inside Out.

This animated movie is the story of 11-year-old Riley and revolves around what goes on inside her head, which is referred to as "the control room." The control room is where choices are made about how to handle emotions and, for Riley—as well as the rest of us—it is staffed by five key emotions or, in this case, characters: Joy, Fear, Disgust, Anger, and Sadness.

In the movie, Riley moves to a new town. On her first day at her new school, Sadness accidentally causes her to cry in front of her class. Joy, who is the boss (because, given a choice, wouldn't we rather be ruled by Joy, than by characters representing Fear, Disgust, Anger, or Sadness?), tries to get rid of Sadness and accidentally knocks the other memories loose, causing Joy to no longer be the leader in the control room.

After a colorful journey, Riley matures, so her emotions begin to all work together with Joy, and she begins to lead a more satisfying (and emotionally complex) life. The three-step shift to gratitude that this story illustrates is:

1. *External*—An event or situation occurs, triggering a negative or difficult emotion, feeling, or thought. (Riley attends a new school.)

2. *Internal*—Self-awareness of the emotions, feelings, or thoughts occurs and an intentional shift to gratitude is made. (Riley is sad and misses her old school and friends. Sadness is now in control.)

3. *External*—Once the shift to gratitude is made, a response is made to the initial event, situation, or trigger by framing the problem, asking questions, making a decision, and taking action. (Riley reconnects with her old schoolmates and makes new friends. Joy takes control again.)

Riley's story shows how the transition from external, to internal, to external plays out. The bottom line is when we consciously shift to gratitude, the resulting external actions are better. The following steps further describe the Three-Step Gratitude Process in action.

Step 1. External: Triggering Event or Situation

An external event takes place, causing you to experience a negative or difficult emotion, feeling, or thought.

- Paul's boss humiliates and belittles him in public.
- Pollyanna is forced to live with her mean aunt, is hit by a car, and loses the use of her legs.
- Malala Yousafzai has a gun pointed at her head.
- I've been pulled off a major client account.

Step 2. Internal: Acknowledging and Shifting

Internally you acknowledge your emotions, feelings, and thoughts. Using a technique that works best for you, you consciously shift to authentic gratitude.

- Paul feels hurt, frustration, and anger. Later, when his internal state changes to gratitude, he better understands himself and his management style and chooses to change his behaviors.

- Pollyanna feels disappointment and uses "the glad game" to see the bright side.

- Malala Yousafzai wants to kill her attacker, but she uses self-distancing to change to a state of peace instead.

- I am angry, defensive, and blaming, but once I remember what I'm grateful for and the great experiences I've had with the clients, I take deep breathes and am able to become calm.

Step 3. External: Taking Action

After the shift to gratitude is made, you take newer, more innovative external actions and the outcomes are often very different.

- Paul leaves his current position and, later, when looking through a gratitude lens, he changes his management behaviors and becomes a better leader. Without the shift: he did not advance and change his own management style.

- With the help of gratitude from the town, Pollyanna engages in rehabilitation, which results in her walking again. Without the shift: she may have not recovered.

- Malala Yousafzai chooses peace, dialogue, and education and wins a Noble Peace Prize. Without the shift: she may have killed or harmed her attacker, or he may have killed or harmed her.

- I asked questions to gain understanding and get valuable feedback. I get the client back and get more work. Without the shift: I may have lost that job and all future jobs arising from that same account, and I wouldn't have received such helpful feedback.

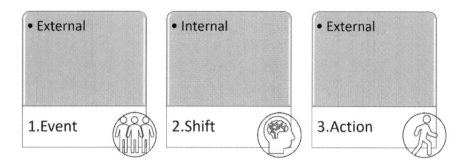

In Paul's case, it took three years to go from negative feelings to reflection using a gratitude lens. By the time he shifted, he had already left the company and they lost a valuable employee.

In Pollyanna's case, it took weeks before she became grateful again, which eventually led to her walking; and Malala Yousafzai shifted out of the negative in seconds and did not try to kill her attacker, an action that may have resulted in her death.

In my case, it seemed like it took forever to react when the account rep told me I was being removed. However, I suspect it was actually less than 30 seconds and I was able to shift to feeling grateful, enabling me to keep my client (and gain two more).

How can you make the Three-Step Gratitude Process happen faster so that different choices become available, giving you a better outcome? By strengthening your gratitude muscle through a deliberate practice, and by adapting the practice to your needs.

Recognize that this does not mean repeating the same action for 10,000 hours in an effort to build your gratitude muscle. Rather, it is a matter of adapting and adjusting how you practice gratitude, and this is process that, in addition to being used at work, can also be applied at home.

Susan came home after a 14-hour day mentally and physically exhausted. Her husband greeted her and proudly explained how he had been helping and cleaned up. However, she instantly noticed the dirty dishes in the sink and became angry. (Step 1: external event)

Remembering her gratitude practice, Susan focused on how she loved her husband and how he did try in his own way. This shifted her focus away from the anger. (Step 2, internal shift)

Susan smiled lovingly at her husband and said in a joking way, "Seems like the maid forgot the dishes today," and happily started doing them. (Step 3, external action)

Her husband joined in and the rest of the evening was good, a result that Susan believes her shift to gratitude created because it enabled her to avoid a fight, and what would likely be a very unpleasant evening.

These three simple steps have helped hundreds of people in both their personal and business lives. The key is to practice them and adapt them so they work for you.

Each of the steps present unique challenges, and some are easier while others may feel harder. Here are some suggestions that have helped others move faster through each step:

Step 1. External: Identifying Triggers

- Learn your specific triggers by recording situations and noticing people who tend to evoke negative emotions
- Practice awareness and mindfulness
- Ask for feedback, either informally or formally
- Seek clarity on your values and beliefs

Step 2. Internal: Shifting to Gratitude

- Take three deep and slow breaths
- Self-distance, refer to yourself in the third person

- Ask your key question or statement (What am I grateful for? Will it matter in 5 years? What could make this worse?)
- Have a physical reminder of gratitude to see or touch

Step 3. External Action

Replace the negative action with a positive one by choosing to:

- Do nothing
- Say or do something different
- Think differently
- Move away from or towards the situation
- Use different voice tone, gestures, or body language

In chapter 11, there are many ideas you can you can use to adapt and practice gratitude. So, if something isn't working or your advancement has slowed down, try something else.

I attribute my ability to quickly shift to being immersed in gratitude for hours during the time I was writing this book. I am fairly sure I would not have responded as positively to my situation if I had not been immersed and running gratitude as a background process.

Takeaways

This chapter shows by example how the shift to gratitude changes the outcome of situations. A practice of gratitude can be learned, practiced, and improved, so a shift happens more quickly and results in different (and better) choices of action.

- Shifting to gratitude can take seconds or it can take decades.

- The Three-Step Gratitude Process outlines the process required to shift to gratitude. It starts externally, then an internal shift, and ends with external action.

- The goal is to shorten the time it takes to make this shift whenever possible because, the faster the shift, the healthier and more productive the results.

- The shift is not denying the negative, rather embracing it and moving forward.

The following reflections can help you better understand and begin to apply the Three-Step Gratitude Process.

Internal Reflection and Discussion

1. In what areas have you completed 10,000 hours or practice? Was it a conscious practicing? Do you consider yourself an expert in these areas now? How long have you been practicing gratitude?

2. Over the course of your life, how has your gratitude practice changed or shifted, consciously or unconsciously?

3. Take a difficult situation you have experienced and map out the Three-Step Gratitude Process, including the result. Did a shift to gratitude occur? If not, consider the different actions you might have taken to achieve different outcomes.

External Reflection and Discussion

1. Mentoring is widely recognized as a way to advance and learn something specific. What mentoring have you been a part of? What would you like to be mentored in?

2. Who are the mentors of people that you consider to be leaders?

3. Using the Three-Step Gratitude Process, map out a typical, yet difficult team scenario (a missed deadline, being over budget, dealing with an angry customer) and consider the different outcomes based on whether the shift to gratitude is made or not.

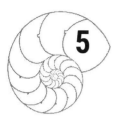

How Culture and Style Impact Giving

*We are human because our ancestors learned to share their
food and their skills in an honored network of obligation.*

Richard Leaky

Americans give lots. In fact, in 2015 alone, they gave an estimated $373.25 billion to charity, the highest reported total in 60 years.
That same year, 64.5 million adults volunteered 7.9 billion hours of
time, valued at $175 billion. Roughly 20 percent of all adults in the
U.S. were formally recognized as volunteers in 2015, donating, on
average, 24 hours of time and giving $1,150 a year to charity.

Time and money are both ways to measure giving, but they are
not the whole picture. How a person or organization shows gratitude
matters too. As cultures overlap and intersect and the demographics
of the U.S. workforce transform, leading with gratitude prompts and
supports change in a more positive way.

Pay It Forward

Gratitude is already built into parts of our society, beyond the
obvious day of thanks: Thanksgiving. For instance, Pay It Forward is
a movement that comes from feelings of generosity and its concept

is simple. *Do something good for someone else without any expectation of anything in return.*

It may be something as small as paying for coffee or covering the highway toll for the person behind you; or it could involve something larger, like paying for a college student's tuition because they supported you by taking care of your elderly parents. Based on a book and subsequently a movie, Pay It Forward is a form of giving and caring for others. It is a natural extension of gratitude.

This notion first became popular back in the 1950s, when science fiction writer Robert A. Heinlein wrote:

The banker reached into the folds of his gown, pulled out a single credit note. But eat first—a full belly steadies the judgment. Do me the honor of accepting this as our welcome to the newcomer.

His pride said no; his stomach said yes! Don took it and said, "Uh, thanks! That's awfully kind of you. I'll pay it back, first chance."

"Instead, pay it forward to some other brother who needs it."

In this case, Heinlein was mirroring what he believed in—giving without expecting anything in return. The Heinlein Society is named after him and is a humanitarian organization based on the concept of paying it forward in the form of scholarships, education, blood drives, and giving away books.

Heinlein himself paid it forward by mentoring Ray Bradbury, a man who, like Heinlein, also became a classic science fiction writer. Bradbury paid it forward as well by helping other aspiring writers, asking them to also pay it forward to others.

Here's an excerpt taken from *Dandelion Wine*, a novel written by Bradbury:

How do I thank Mr. Jonas, he wondered, for what he's done? How do I thank him, how pay him back? No way, no way at all.

You just can't pay. What then? What? Pass it on somehow, he thought, pass it on to someone else. Keep the chain moving. Look around, find someone, and pass it on. That was the only way. When people feel gratitude, they are more generous and give more, time and money.

When paying it forward, the more we give, the more we get back. I know this personally, and I hear it repeatedly from those steeped in gratitude.

Gender and Gratitude

In the U.S., men are socialized to be autonomous, competitive, and achievement-oriented—all individual pursuits. The problem arises when these individual pursuits become more important than collaboration, caring, and community building. (I know some businesses that hire only college athletes because they know how to work in teams.) In these cases, gratitude doesn't provide as much value.

Women, on the other hand, are very different. Several studies conclude that, because gratitude creates stronger social bonds, relationships, and caring, women often see its value and express it more frequently than men.

Generally speaking, women are also more emotional than men. For instance, many studies show that women experience emotions more intensely, more frequently, and in a more complex way than their male counterparts. They communicate, collaborate, and express emotions more often (with the one exception of anger) as well.

Women are also typically better at adapting and regulating their emotions based on situation. In a meeting that has become emotional, for instance, it will typically be a woman who takes action to regulate the emotions in the room and bring it back on track.

Human resources departments, which are responsible for all things related to people—salary, benefits, career, hiring, firing, performance reviews—are also predominately run by women, with 76 percent of the managers being female according to the U.S. Department of Labor.

Age and Gratitude

Another factor to consider is age. Many studies show that aging, maturing, and having more life experiences increases a person's gratitude. However, one study found that 76 percent of millennials show gratitude or thankfulness weekly, roughly the same amount as other generations.

Millennials are generalized as being fast movers, well-connected, and transparent. Many live their lives on social media, so we know their relationship status (studies show they get married less), employment situation, and even what they had for breakfast.

At work, Millennials care more about performance and merit than they do longevity and salary. They are self-confident and want their work to count and be challenged. They seek ways to advance and improve, asking for feedback 50 percent more often than any other age group in the workplace.

Work/life balance is also important to millennials. They prefer more vacation time, flexibility, and experiences (like traveling) over a salary increase. They like to work for companies like the West Coast tech giants—Google, Apple, and Facebook—that share their social causes. They're not loyal to companies who don't share their social beliefs, and they want to make a difference in the world.

"Thank you is over used and not meaningful," one millennial said to me, highlighting that this age group also typically don't just do something because it is a norm. It must have meaning.

All of the combined shows that the key to attracting and retaining millennials is creating a culture of authentic appreciation that supports meaningful work, work that challenges and advances society. Gratitude is an attribute desirable to millennials.

Culture and Gratitude

While the U.S. is culturally diverse, there is a mainstream culture that has influenced business here for centuries. This culture has been predominantly male (only 4 percent of the Fortune 500 companies are run by women) and white Anglo-Saxon Protestant. This results in the workforce being driven by their values and behaviors, many of which are competition and achievement-based.

However, two major factors will disrupt this mainstream business culture in the near future. One is the changing workplace demographics. For instance, approximately 70 million baby boomers are expected to retire in the upcoming years according to the U.S. Census Bureau.

Additionally, more states are seeing higher non-white populations (New Mexico is 48 percent Hispanic and Lawrence, Massachusetts is 73.8 percent of the population is Hispanic or Latino according to Pew Research). The U.S. Census adds that there are over 26 cities in this country where 50 percent or more of the population is black or African American.

Another demographic change is related to gender. According to a 2014 research report commissioned by American Express OPEN, more than 9.4 million businesses are owned by women, accounting for 31 percent of all privately held firms. Of those, 2.9 percent are owned by women of color.

The second major factor impacting the U.S. business culture is worldwide connectedness. Language barriers are disappearing with global technology advances. Transparency and access are available almost everywhere.

It's unclear exactly what new mainstream culture will emerge in the future, or if there will be such a thing as a mainstream culture at all. The only guarantee is that it *is* changing.

This makes the need for a universal value and practice of gratitude even more important because gratitude can bridge these changes in a positive way rather than instigating the negative characteristics commonly associated with change: resistance, belittling, mistrust, and anger…emotions that typically cause humans to operate out of fear.

In today's mainstream culture, the belief is that if you work hard, you will advance. It is okay to question and challenge authority, and personal responsibility is key. Communication is direct and fact-oriented in today's culture too, with innovation and the entrepreneurial spirt highly valued.

Everyone is equal, relationships are informal, and we call our bosses by their first name. But personal space is important, so don't stand too close (no closer than two feet according to *Kiss, Bow, or Shake hands* by Morrison and Conway).

Professor Geert Hofstede created one of the most researched and most utilized national cultural measurement tools called the Hofstede Cultural Index. This index uses six categories to rate national cultures on a scale of 1 to 100. With over 100 national value ratings and translated into 20 different languages, the two scales of measurement most related to gender and gratitude are Masculine-Femininity and Individualism-Collectivism.

On his website, Professor Geert Hofstede's describes masculinity versus femininity:

The Masculinity side of this dimension represents a preference in society for achievement, heroism, assertiveness and material rewards for success. Society at large is more competitive. Its opposite, femininity, stands for a preference for cooperation, modesty, caring for the weak and quality of life. Society at large is more consensus-oriented. In the business context Masculinity versus Femininity is sometimes also related to as "tough versus tender" cultures.

According to Hofstede, the U.S. culture scores high in masculinity, at 61 percent. This means that this society is driven by competition, achievement, and striving to be the best.

Here are the characteristics of individualism versus collectivism, again from Geert's website:

The high side of this dimension, called individualism, can be defined as a preference for a loosely knit social framework in which individuals are expected to take care of only themselves and their immediate families. Its opposite, collectivism, represents a preference for a tightly knit framework in society in which individuals can expect their relatives or members of a particular in-group to look after them in exchange for unquestioning loyalty. A society's position on this dimension is reflected in whether people's self-image is defined in terms of "I" or "we."

The U.S. has one of the highest scores for individualism in the world at a 91. This places the focus on one person, the individual, and not the entire team.

Gratitude is a behavior that supports and encourages the opposite of this. It promotes collectivism, which is community focused and requires collaboration and teamwork. It also builds bonds and loyalty. So, when individual behavior is the predominate culture and a driving factor, gratitude is not valued.

The following chart provides more information about the relative characteristics of the U.S. work culture based on Geert's findings.

USA CULTURE CHARACTERISTICS

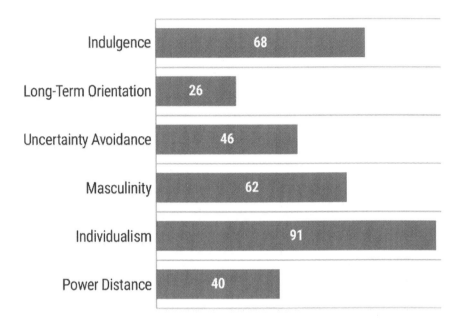

Different Management Styles

Making people cry, always speaking up first, talking over others, and not listening were just a few of the complaints people had about Kevin A, a highly competent manager with a reputation for obtaining results in difficult and complex situations.

Kevin A's background and behaviors fit the profile of the mainstream work culture. He played contact sports and was in the military. He was highly competitive, aggressive, and very direct. For him, emotions had no place in business. "Business is not personal," was his motto. He was also known to say, "Get over it" and "Business is a game to be won."

However, as Kevin A's company grew and become more diverse, employing talent from all over the world, the behaviors that had previously helped him achieve success were no longer acceptable. After 10 years, his promotions stalled. Kevin A became resentful and unhappy about his lack of advancement in the company that once celebrated and promoted his work style.

Many people could see his brilliance and wanted him to succeed, but it wasn't until Kevin A opened himself up to seeing the impact of his behaviors (and their impact on others) that he was able to change. The changes he made were simple—talking less and listening more—but difficult for him. It wasn't until he appreciated those who wanted to help him and stayed open to their feedback that he started to change.

Kevin B, on the other hand, lacked empathy and didn't care about other people, their opinions, or their jobs. Subsequently, he was let go every year-and-a-half from key positions. Not because he lacked competence, but because he hadn't developed trust with other team members. So, whenever a layoff occurred, it was always easy to make Kevin B the first to go, though he didn't initially realize that his lack of empathy was to blame for his earlier-than-desired departure.

Kevin C is yet another variation, a man whose physical presence and ability to dominate others' personal space made people fear him. As a manager, Kevin C's staff would not open up to him. That is, until he learned to stop talking, sit back in his chair, and actually listen to what they had to say.

In all of these cases, the behavior changes and gratitude behaviors the three Kevin's began to use at work spilled over into their personal lives. For instance, years later, Kevin A shared with me how, because of his gratitude work, he had been able to deliver a loving message to his wife at an anniversary celebration that brought tears to everyone's eyes. This was something he never would've done before he learned to appreciate others.

Initially, Kevin A, Kevin B, and Kevin C were common examples of the mainstream work culture. They all had competitive and aggressive behaviors, creating major issues for them in the increasingly diverse workplace.

When left unchecked, a lack of gratitude results in toxic workplaces. Thus, gratitude was a behavior and way of being that helped them all remain true to themselves, yet still be able to work effectively in diverse businesses.

Gratitude and Individual Personality Styles

At home I am a nice guy, but I don't want the world to know.
Humble people, I've found, don't get very far.

Muhammad Ali

The advantages of personality tests are their ability to provide a general sense of who a person is, how they work, how they behave, and how they're viewed by others. That makes them useful when used to hire people, determine compatibility, and figure out how to help them work together better. These assessments also offer common, nonjudgmental language for us to use when we want to talk about softer areas, like communication and emotions.

The downside of personality tests is that they create stereotypes and apply labels. We are more complex than any one label and most people don't fit into the categories perfectly. So, the questions we must ask when presented with the results of our own personality tests are: How much is this like me and, conversely, how much is this *not* like me?

The DISC tool is one of the simplest and most intuitive personality tests to use and interpret as it doesn't require certification or a deep understanding. The concept was first developed in 1928 from a book by William Marston titled *Emotions of Normal People*. According to Marston, there are four different behavioral patterns:

1. **D** for Direct (originally called Dominance)

2. **I** for Influence (originally called Inducement)

3. **S** for Steady (originally called Submission)

4. **C** for Conscientious (originally called Compliance)

An individual's primary behavior quadrant in the DISC assessment determines and impacts his or her motivations, communication style, decision making strategies, problem solving processes, and conflict-resolving behaviors. It can also impact gratitude behaviors, such as how they give and would like to receive gratitude.

For instance, I (Influence) and S (Steady) are more people-oriented and extroverted. So, a strong "I" loves public recognition of gratitude, with lots of people and lots of conversational interactions. One company performed a flash mob to thank an employee for a job well done, exactly what an "I" would love!

A strong "S" wants to make sure that, however the thanks is given or received, it was fair; that everyone who deserves it is recognized so no feathers are ruffled and no one is left out. Holding a public and harmonious event that everyone can agree on, attend, and be happy about is what a strong "S" would love.

D (Direct) and C (Conscientious) people are the opposite as they are more task-oriented and introverted. A strong "D" prefers to give and receive gratitude in a manner that is to the point and not lingering. No long flowery speeches for the "D," just a clear and concise, "Thanks for going above and beyond and helping the support team this weekend," and then let's move on.

Fast-Paced, Verbal	
D = Direct Direct Decisive Driven Focused on results Prefers action over planning Long term Big picture vision Seeks challenges Takes risks **Task-Oriented**	**I = Influence** Inspirational Intuitive Seeks constant stimulation Enjoys interacting with others Thrives in social environments Thirsts for adventure Optimistic Persuasive Fun Positive energy **People-Oriented**
C = Conscientious Concise Cautious Correct Achieves complete accuracy Questions processes Ensures things are done properly Systematic, detail-oriented, efficient Makes practical decisions Logical analysis Prefers to work independently Even-tempered nature Remains objective	**S = Steady** Sympathetic Sincere Supportive Restores harmony Minimizes conflict Creates calm, safe environments Friendly, compassionate Patiently listens Builds deep, loyal relationships Steadfast friends Practical, tried-and-true, stable Likes familiar, predictable patterns Consistent and reliable outcomes Works behind the scenes
Slower Paced, Verbally, Methodical	

A strong "C" wants to make sure the gratitude is specific and accurate. Word choice is important, as is location and who is or is not present. "Thank you for spending all afternoon with Chris and his team on Saturday to help them resolve the input problem four our most lucrative customer. The patch has been presented and they have closed the problem report."

After taking the DISC test, a graph is provided that shows your strengths and where you lie in each of these four quadrants. The X axis represents your variance between being people-oriented and task-based; the Y axis shows where you are in the range between being active (fast paced) and being thoughtful or methodical.

Marston's DISC model is based on his belief that a person can behave in seemingly opposite ways depending on the situation and circumstance. In other words, someone may be more of an "I" (Influential) at home and a "C" (Conscientious) at work.

For instance, one manager swore a lot at home. As in, a curse word was used in almost every sentence or phrase. However, she only swore about once a year to her staff, only when she needed to get their attention and emphasize the importance of a situation. She could turn this behavior on and off as the situation required.

Marston's embrace of all behavior patterns was included in the groundbreaking heroine he created for DC Comics: Wonder Woman. While a fictitious character, Wonder Woman exhibited all four behavior patterns, adapting each one as needed based on the situation.

She was Direct and strong, and Influential in her job of doing good for society while also being feminine, Submissive (Steady), and Conscientious (she paid attention to details and had lots of cool tools). Because all behaviors exist in Wonder Woman, everybody can see themselves in her and, thus, relate.

Many years after I delivered a DISC workshop, Henry, a manager in a software company, stopped me in the hallway to say that he uses what he learned from DISC every day and it has made his job easier. I only knew Henry from that one workshop, so I had no idea what he meant and embarrassingly had to ask.

Henry told me that, when he learned to focus on the behaviors and not the person, it made his job easier because he stopped judging individuals and taking things personal. When a team member was late to a meeting and it was his job to provide feedback, for instance, Henry focused on the behavior of being late rather than judging the person.

This kept Henry's brain out of threat mode and into problem-solving mode. It also changed the problem itself. Instead of focusing on the problem of someone disrespecting him, he solved the behavior problem of someone being late. This kept Henry and his team in a more positive place.

Regardless of what personality tools you might use, consider how each type of person likes to give and receive gratitude. That way, when planning an event or acknowledging contributions or achievements, you're able to take the individual's personality type into account so the accolades are more likely be accepted.

Takeaways

There is a major shift in business due to changes in the mainstream workforce. These changes will create many challenges for businesses, such as attracting and keeping millennial workers. Thus, it is important for companies to consider all factors (age, gender, demographics, and individual personality styles) and to proactively plan for the team and organizational culture they want.

Shifting cultures is one of the hardest things to manage and has been the death of many businesses. Committing to gratitude will ease cultural and organizational changes by appreciating the workforce in way that is meaningful to them.

Here are some more key points to take into consideration:

- There are two main contributing factors to the changing U.S. business culture: 1) changing demographics and 2) worldwide connectiveness. Both can benefit by embracing gratitude in the workplace.

- Understanding how preferences for giving and receiving appreciation differ is the first step. The more a leader can adapt to the individual, the easier it is for him or her to acknowledge and receive gratitude.

- Understanding the composition of the workforce—its specific cultural traits, age ranges, genders, and beliefs—will help when creating a deliberate culture of gratitude.

Internal Reflection and Discussion

1. What demographic groups do you belong or relate to most? What are the generalizations about that group and gratitude? Do you fit this generalization?

2. How do you, as an employee, prefer to receive appreciation and gratitude?

3. As a leader or manager, when, why, and how do you give and show appreciation and gratitude?

External Reflection and Discussion

1. How would you describe your team or organization's culture? Do you consider it mainstream? Revolutionary? Supportive? Why?

2. How does your team or organization practice gratitude, appreciation, and inclusion, both formally and informally?

3. What demographic changes are occurring or will occur in your organization? What does each demographic want and/or need in regard to appreciation and gratitude?

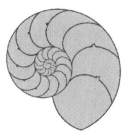

PART 3
A IS FOR ANALYSIS

Not everything that looks like gratitude is gratitude. Gratitude has several close cousin's that we'll explore. We'll also review some of the risks and barriers of gratitude.

The GLAD Tool is an approach for analyzing gratitude similar to what many organizations are already doing. It encourages the use of data, facts, and analysis to add in gratitude, making it helpful when coaching others and for teams interested in creating plans and strategies for success.

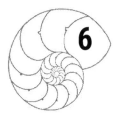

Mindfulness, Optimism, Happiness, and Thank You

6

Gratitude is not only the greatest of virtues,
but the parent of all the others.

Cicero

The faculty of bringing back a wandering attention over and
over again is the very root of judgment, character, and will.

William James

Mindfulness *or* Gratitude?

Gratitude has many cousins, some of which include happiness, optimism, reciprocity, trust, and mindfulness. Like all familial relationships, each of these share similar DNA.

All of these cousins are learnable skills and muscles that can be strengthened. All can be self-managed, and the more they are practiced, the easier that management becomes. All are also complementary to each other, making them worth adding to your gratitude practice and plan.

However, as in any family, their relationship is not quite black and white as all of these cousins are subjective. This makes them challenging to define, research, measure, teach, and learn as what might make one person happy can drive another nuts. For example, some people prefer a long, deliberate, detailed, fair, and comprehensive review of a new product while others want only the high-level benefits.

These cousins also vary in terms of how deeply and how often individuals experience them. To better illustrate this, picture where each would appear on a spectrum.

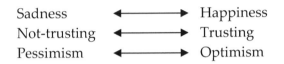

These sliding-scale states can be measured for individuals, teams, organizations, and situations—and they can vary from minute to minute.

Gratitude and mindfulness are more closely related than the others because each is a path, gateway, or set of tools that can be used for building on the other. However, they aren't the same and it's like asking the age-old question: Which comes first, the chicken or the egg? Does mindfulness appear before gratitude or vice versa?

Jon Kabat-Zinn, founder of a popular mediation practice MBSR (Mindfulness-Based Stress Reduction), defines mindfulness as, "The awareness that emerges through paying attention on purpose, in the present moment, and nonjudgmentally to the unfolding of the experience." Put simply, when you're mindful, you're not worrying about the past or planning what you need to do next. You are only focused on what is right now.

The irony of this definition is that your goal when being mindful is not to keep your mind "full," but rather to empty it of any thoughts that pull you into the past or future. It is to keep yourself aware and focused on the current situation.

There are many ways to be mindful and meditation is the pre-dominant method most associated with this practice because meditation retrains and strengthens your attention.

Being hypnotized or using self-hypnosis can also create a state of mindfulness, as can walking and other types of movement. This is contrary to the fast-paced environment most of us live in, with no time for anything, too much to do, always multitasking, and participating in a stress-filled business world.

Together, this lifestyle screams for us to find a way to bring about being mindful quickly so we can reduce stress, increase energy, and focus attention on what matters most. But how much mindfulness is necessary to create these types of effects?

Just ten minutes of mindfulness can minimize the damage multitasking causes to concentration. Eight minutes of mindfulness can keep the mind from wandering for a short while. If you want more lasting benefits, this requires an ongoing practice of some form of meditation. This isn't a natural state for most adults, but, like gratitude, it can be learned.

Babies are born mindful, though, as we age, we become less mindful due to socialization. That said, retaining our innate mindfulness and raising mindful children are both gaining in popularity. Meditation is also replacing detention as more and more schools are bringing mindfulness into the classroom.

There are many benefits to this as studies are finding that children are more focused and less confrontational when they are mindful. Terri, a friend of mine, teaches this skill to children by asking them to concentrate on their rhythmical breathing and stay focused in the present while following the movement of a toy called a Hoberman Sphere (a colorful sphere that expands and contracts).

Mindfulness has become an accepted strategic tool used to improve leadership effectiveness and employee health in businesses as well. Meditation centers and mindfulness practices are popping up in many workplaces, with companies like Google offering mindfulness training to all its employees (and the rest of the world through its Search Inside Yourself Leadership Institute).

Gabriele, an executive coach and organizational development consultant, has studied and practiced meditation and mindfulness for over 20 years. She reports that, over the past five years, more and more of her corporate coaching clients have requested mindfulness to improve their effectiveness and well-being as leaders.

As a coach and consultant, Gabriele deals with complex organizational relationships in a world filled with increasing disturbances, distractions, and ever-growing uncertainties. Thus, her clients draw more and more on meditation and centering practices.

They also request guidance in regard to leadership spirit. Senior executives bring questions like "How do I stay inspirational and positive when I no longer see the fruits of my actions or believe in the strategy?" to the table as they face relentless change, reorganization, and volatility in strategic focus.

Gabriele says that she aspires to be and create "islands of peace and sanity" for these business leaders and individuals who desire to become and remain centers of calmness, clarity, and creativity among the uncertainty. Meditation, mindfulness, and centering practices are a core part of her business.

For some, being mindful isn't easy and meditation is a loaded word, mainly because of its association with other religions. Plus, not all organizations and people are open to mindfulness and meditation practices. Gratitude helps bridge that gap.

Gratitude is generally easier to do, accept, and creates less resistance. Asking a question like, "What am I grateful for?" can pull a person into being mindful and gratitude itself is a more generic, less religion-associated, and less-loaded word.

Unlike meditation, gratitude can be done with eyes open in the here and now. It can also prompt action, whereas mindfulness alone does not. In fact, there is a movement of linking mindfulness with action.

Thich Nhat Hanh, a Vietnamese monk, calls it *engaged Buddhism* and says that action coming from the place of mindfulness is compassion. He strongly advocates for it by saying:

> *Mindfulness must be engaged.... Once we see that something needs to be done, we must take action. Seeing and action go together. Otherwise, what is the point in seeing?*

Put another way, mindfulness involves just "being" since, when you're being mindful, you're encouraged to swat away all of your "should've," "could've," and "must-do-now" thoughts. Gratitude is different because it is an underlying state of being that creates positive, creative, and innovative actions, solutions, and results.

Ironically, when we become mindful, we also become more grateful. And when we are more grateful, we become more mindful. Those who are regular practitioners of meditation and mindfulness say that gratitude has a way of sneaking in.

So, in the end, it is just like the chicken and the egg. It doesn't matter which comes first, mindfulness or gratitude. Instead, what matters most is that you start with either of these so you can ultimately get where it is you want to go.

Mindfulness *and* Gratitude

Managers are frequently required to have juggling-like skills. They interact with many diverse functions and teams and work at producing different levels of outcomes. Being mindful allows for nonjudgmental observation in these situations without assigning any immediate subjective assessment. In the moment, the situation is not defined as good, bad, hard, or easy. It just is what it is.

Mindfulness provides the flexibility to enter problem-solving mode and choose from among the best actions rather than being stuck in reflexive mental habits or emotions that limit your options. This is not to say that cultivating mindfulness means that emotions and feeling should be denied, repressed, or ignored. Rather, at that moment of decision, the goal is to observe them and allow action from less constrained, more expanded choices.

It's similar to being in an emergency situation and choosing to do lifesaving actions now and dealing with the emotional impact of the event later. Mindfulness in that moment of choice expands the possibilities of action.

There are many ways to learn to become more mindful, you just need to figure out what works for you. Combined with mindfulness, gratitude adds a dimension of appreciation for other people and other situations. It is the catalyst for caring and empathy.

Mindfulness also sets up gratitude; it is a tool for becoming grateful. A gratitude practice in the workplace has a more direct impact on the actions of individuals, teams, and organizations.

Happiness

I believe that the very purpose of our existence
Is to seek happiness.

Dalai Lama

Whether you are religious or not, happiness is important. Happiness is a right and a belief firmly implanted in our culture. Even the U.S. constitution mentions the right to "the pursuit of happiness."

In a September 2015 *Forbes* interview, Shawn Riegsecker, CEO of Centro—the company *Fortune* ranked number one best place to work among all midsize American companies—says, "Happiness is the new ROI [return on investment]." This philosophy has resulted in one of the highest rankings possible on the employee review site, Glassdoor.

Shawn has created a manifesto for governing Centro which includes employees' happiness, growth, and well-being. It also calls for each person to be responsible for his or her own improvements, as well as those of the company and the community. This includes being grateful for opportunities and is a positive and appealing manifesto for many, particularly his millennial staff.

In today's culture, the pursuit of happiness has become pervasive both personally and professionally. Some say it's the short-term focus on bottom-line profits and earnings that is promoting this movement. In my opinion, in a decade or so, happiness as a value will become part of the new mainstream in business, as well as making a greater appearance in our personal lives as well.

"Ninety percent of our happiness comes from and can be predicted by the way our brain processes the external world," explains Harvard University Psychologist Shawn Achor, CEO of Good Think Inc., the organization where he researches and teaches positive psychology. According to Achor, happiness is a feeling and emotion that is pervasive worldwide.

He also talks about the "happiness advantage" because, when we are happy at work, our productivity increases by 31 percent. Employees also perform more intelligently, are more creative, and are more successful in achieving their goals when happiness exists.

Organizations have long used the carrot-and-stick approach to motivation. They pay higher amounts and give more rewards (the carrot) to motivate employees. They also pay less and remove rewards when performance is poor (the stick).

In the book *Drive*, author Daniel Pink suggests that the carrot-and-stick approach is still effective for repetitive-type work. However, when the work is non-repetitive, motivation must come from an internal desire. It must come from doing meaningful work.

Meaningful work, according to Pink, is work that allows people to be autonomous. It involves working toward mastery and is tied in to a larger purpose or goal (hopefully, the same purpose or goal of the organization). Ultimately, when employees are motivated, they are happy.

Brené Brown adds to the conversation in a July 15, 2011, *Forbes* interview, in which she says, "I don't have to chase extraordinary moments to find happiness; it is right in front of me if I am paying attention and practicing gratitude." In her research, one of the most amazing discoveries she made was the relationship between joy (happiness) and gratitude as everyone Brown interviewed who described themselves as joyous or joyful had a conscious practice of gratitude.

Thus, gratitude is the key to creating happiness according to Brown (and many other experts for that matter). The more gratitude you have, the more happiness you experience.

Trust and Gratitude

In the leadership section, we highlighted two models with cores based on trust: Covey's *The Speed of Trust* and Lencioni's *The Five Dysfunctions of a Team*. We also showed trust as being measurable in the brain and similar to gratitude in that it is only available when we aren't in survival mode. There are many hypotheses from the scientific and the spiritual communities as to what this means, though the premise held by many is that gratitude enhances trust.

For instance, in one study, a gratitude intervention was conducted with a group of participants before strangers were to play a game together. In the intervention group, meaningful trust behaviors were exhibited and resulted in a trust boost of 17.5 percent, which translated into this group trusting each other more.

This greater level of trust led the participants engaged in the pregame intervention to take more risks, like spending more money. And it was the intervention group that, when playing the games, always won. The figure below illustrates the relationship between gratitude and trust.

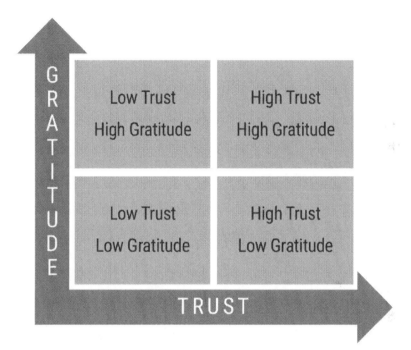

To see this in your own life, think of the person you trust the *least* at work. When he or she asks you to do something, what is your typical response? If you're like most people, you likely either ignore the request or put it on the bottom of your to-do list.

Now, imagine a person you don't trust, but are grateful for (maybe for the work he or she does). If this person asks you to do something, does it change your immediate response?

Alternatively, think of the person you trust *most* at work, and imagine that he or she asks you to do something that is not that appealing or outside your normal job. What would your response be?

Typical responses are to do the task, do it in a high-quality way, and do it fast.

Now let's add gratitude to the mix. Think of a person you are grateful for and trust and picture him or her asking you to do something. Does gratitude change how you respond to the request?

In most cases, trust and gratitude are two factors that lead to the highest quality and fastest turnaround times on work requests, regardless of what those requests are. And in my experience running more than 100 workshops, I've learned that, even if we don't know the person who is asking us to do something very well, our gratitude significantly boosts our productivity when we trust him or her. Put simply, gratitude builds and enhances trust.

Gratitude Is Not Optimism

I didn't see it then, but it turned out that getting fired from Apple
was the best thing that could have ever happened to me.

Steve Jobs, 2005

If the project you're working on is a failure, which of these two statements are you more likely to think: "I'm such a failure; I can't do anything right" or "It was just a project; I'll do better next time"?

The first is a pessimistic response that makes the failure personal, turning it into an internal failure. Internal failures sound like this:

- "I can't do this."
- "I'm a pervasive failure."
- "I'm always wrong."
- "I can never do anything right."

The optimist response (the second one) is less personal in nature. Therefore, it takes the failure and makes it more external:

- "I can do this under different circumstances."
- "It is a limited failure."
- "It's just one project."
- "I'll do better next time."

Extensive research shows many physical and mental benefits of optimism. For instance, optimistic people take more risks because they believe that there will eventually be a positive outcome. They anticipate more because the future looks positive, causing them to try harder and practice more often. But optimism also has a downside.

In a TED Talk, researcher Tali Sharot talks about *optimism bias*. Optimism bias is something I struggle with and it is a belief that things will always work out. Customers *will* buy more. I *will* get that promotion.

When you believe that things will always wind up in your favor, no matter what, you're less likely to put actionable plans in place. Plans that can actually get customers to buy more or that involve you doing what you need to do to get that promotion you want.

The more optimistic you are, the less likely you are to accept negative realities. Your behavior becomes riskier and planning falls by the wayside due to the belief that, in the end, it won't matter because it will all be okay. It's like seeing the world through rose-colored glasses.

Overcoming optimism bias requires looking at real or potential negatives and actively doing something to avoid them. This is much different than just sitting idly by and waiting for a positive outcome.

There have been many times in my personal life where optimism bias has caused me problems. For instance, I've stayed in personal and professional relationships much longer than I should have, always believing it would get better, though it never did.

James Stockdale's story highlights optimism bias perfectly. In 1965, during the Vietnam War, he was a Navy commander and had to eject from his plane. Taken as a prisoner of war, Stockdale was repeatedly tortured. Yet, after being rescued, he said this about his experience: "I would prevail in the end and turn the experience into the defining event of my life, which, in retrospect, I would not trade."

When asked who did *not* survive, Stockdale replied, "Oh, that's easy, the optimists. Oh, they were the ones who said, 'We're going to be out by Christmas.' And Christmas would come, and Christmas would go. Then they'd say, 'We're going to be out by Easter.' And Easter would come, and Easter would go. And then Thanksgiving, and then it would be Christmas again. And they died of a broken heart."

Stockdale's story is documented in *Good to Great*, where Collins labeled this the "Stockdale Paradox." The Stockdale Paradox involves holding two seemingly opposite views to be true: (1) having the ability to have faith it will work out and (2) to confront the brutal facts of your current reality.

Stockdale sums it up this way: "You must never confuse faith that you will prevail in the end—which you can never afford to lose—with the discipline to confront the most brutal facts of your current reality, whatever they might be." Stockdale calls it faith when you can see the reality of the world (good or bad) and not blindly believe that it will be okay and everything will just work out.

The impact of these types of scenarios can be broken down into three groups:

1. *Gratitude Impact.* Accepts responsibly, learns from error, plans to do something different, different results become possible.

2. *Optimistic Impact.* Accepts responsibility, hopes it will get better, does not dig into the error, receives the same results the next time.

3. *Pessimistic Impact.* Does not accept full responsibility, less engaged, no improvement, blames others, and keeps doing the same thing the same way.

The figure below shows how gratitude and optimism could have played out in each of these cases.

Gratitude versus Optimism: Prisoners' Situation		
Thought	**Gratitude Response**	**Optimism Response**
I'm alive.	Grateful for life.	Of course I am.
I've lost my freedom.	Plan for freedom.	I'll be out by Easter.
My jailors are cruel.	Manage my behaviors; learn theirs.	They'll change.

The same three impacts apply in business. For instance, the next figure shows how gratitude, optimism, and pessimism could play out in a situation where an employee made an error.

Gratitude versus Optimism: Work-Related Error			
Thought	**Gratitude**	**Optimism**	**Pessimist**
I made an error.	I can learn from it and improve.	It won't happen again.	It's my fault; I'm stupid.
I have a job.	I will plan for improving.	That's great. There's nothing for me to do.	It's a bad job.

It's amazing how simple thoughts can impact and potentially change the outcome of a situation. These are extreme cases on the end of their spectrum, but the reality is that all of these thoughts may happen in the same situation. You may start with "it's not my fault" and then transition to "it won't happen again" before finally arriving at "I can learn from this."

As an underlying attribute, gratitude can be combined with optimism or pessimism. Put another way, people can be grateful optimists or grateful pessimists. (I call myself a "realistic optimist," a more familiar phrase than grateful optimist.) The key is understanding which predominate approach you will use to resolve the situation and move forward.

When you use gratitude as an underlying base, you don't step over, ignore, or deny facts, no matter how bad or abysmal they might be. Gratitude (and mindfulness) demands that you accept the present reality, though it is not optimism or happiness; yet they all exist on the same side of the brain. Gratitude is simply a base you can use to create happiness, trust, and optimism.

Reciprocity Is Not Gratitude

Gratitude unlocks the fullness of life. It turns what we have into enough, and more. It turns denial into acceptance, chaos into order, confusion into clarity... It turns problems into gifts, failures into success, the unexpected into perfect timing, and mistakes into important events. Gratitude makes sense of our past, brings peace for today, and creates a vision for tomorrow.

Melody Beattie

Gratitude is a basic virtue sometimes called a "cultural lubricant" because it is a cycle of giving that keeps society going. Bartering is reciprocity, payment in exchange for product or service.

Though they are closely related, there is a clear difference between the two.

If you receive payment for a job, you feel obligated to reciprocate and do the work. That is reciprocity. Give and take. Stores use reciprocity all the time by offering discounts, free items, and assisting you so that you will, in turn, feel obligated to make a purchase. Scratch my back, I'll scratch yours.

Home-based direct marketing businesses, at their core, rely on reciprocity to survive. If I invite you to my house and feed you, you feel obligated to order the products I sell, whether those products are jewelry, pocketbooks, or plastic food storage containers.

Research tells us that reciprocity is wired into our DNA and can be manipulated to get people to do what we want. Advertisers and marketers have known this for ages and rely on it for their gain.

For instance, a 30-second Super Bowl commercial costs about $5 million. However, the company is counting on you to feel so good after seeing it that you unconsciously return the favor and purchase its product.

In *Influence: The Psychology of Persuasion,* a book considered to be one of the most important on influencing, author Robert Cialdini combines science with practical advice about how to influence others. Reciprocity is one of the key approaches he discusses.

After reading the book several times and trying reciprocity myself, I was shocked at how easy it is to influence (or manipulate) others. My eyes were opened wide and I could see so many intentional or conscious uses of reciprocity.

As a project manager, I learned that offering free food in exchange for attending our meetings helped get people there. Learning about reciprocity also helped tamper my optimism bias and see interactions in a whole new light.

Here are a few fairly common sayings that many of us have heard (if not used ourselves), proving that reciprocity is still alive and well:

- "Quid pro quo"
- "Share and share alike"
- "Tit for tat"
- "A favor for a favor"
- "One good turn deserves another"
- "Treat others as you would treat yourself"
- "The more you give, the more you receive"

Napoleon Hill, author of the classic book *Think and Grow Rich*, calls reciprocity "a universal law of the marketplace, which Nature herself will reckon if it is bent/broken long enough!"

Ralph Waldo Emerson writes this about reciprocity: "In the order of nature we cannot render benefits to those from whom we receive them, or only seldom. But the benefit we receive must be rendered again, line for line, deed for deed, cent for cent, to somebody."

Both Emerson and Hill can rest easy knowing that what they made famous, the idea of reciprocity, can now be proven with science. The need for reciprocating actions and feelings is hard-wired into our brains.

Three Meanings for "Thank You"

The phrase "thank you" can have several different meanings. I've identified three that are commonly used in U.S. culture. They are: reciprocity, politeness, and gratitude.

When a "thank you" is offered out of reciprocity, it means that something was given to you, so now you feel obligated to give something in return. For example, if you need better support by an IT department and that department needs access to a person you know, reciprocity is a form of trading organizational currencies.

A "thank you" used as politeness is an automatic, unconscious response based on cultural conditioning. It is a habit that is repeated as often as 50 times a day (or more). *Thank you for stopping by! Thank you for shopping here!*

A polite thank you can also be a signal that a transaction is completed or, in conversation, a technique used to stop or avoid further conversation. (Personally, it is how I choose to end telemarketers' phone calls, by sharply saying "thank you" and hanging up the phone.)

Children are taught early on to say thank you for gifts received, even if they don't like them! A habit overdone in cultures like the United States and Japan, in other cultures, like India and Germany, it is inappropriate to thank someone for doing what is their responsibility.

Ironically though, in the U.S.—a highly thanking culture—we are much less inclined to thank those whom we work with on a daily basis. Case in point: only 10 percent of people thank someone at work every day as opposed to 40 percent who give thanks to those in their personal life.

The third type, offering a thank you out of gratitude, is merely an expression of appreciation. There is no agenda and no intent to receive something in return. A gratuitous thank you is offered out of nothing more than positivity and good will and the more you give thanks from a place of true authentic gratitude, the more those feelings of positivity are returned to you.

Giving something without any expectation of anything in return is gratitude. Yet, even when something is given in gratitude, there is still usually an unexpected desire for reciprocation.

If you go above and beyond in your job, for instance, as your employer, I will be grateful and give you more—more money, more responsibility, more perks, and more bonuses. In return, this can motivate (or obligate) you to do more.

A simple example: a manager was given access to a monthly proprietary company report that typically only executives are allowed to see. Feeling obligated, the manager always read it (even though it took about three hours of the manager's already booked time), afterward thanking the executive who forwarded it to him.

Because the manager always thanked the executive for the privilege of seeing the report, this prompted the executive to keep sending it. This document added nothing of value to the manager's job or future career, but they were locked in a cycle of reciprocity that had become burdensome. When the manager stopped thanking the executive, the report stopped being forwarded.

Now look at your own life. What meaning is behind most of *your* "thank you's"? Additionally, how can you differentiate between the different meanings when someone is offering appreciation to you?

It's not easy at times and will typically be colored by how you perceive the person appreciating you. If you have an excellent relationship with your manager, for instance, and she thanks you for a job well done, you may immediately believe that it is given from a point of gratitude. However, another person may have a terrible relationship with the same manager and, when they receive a thank-you, believe they are only being thanked because the manager wants something from them or is being polite.

From the time I was little, saying "thank you" was what nice people do. Thus, it became ingrained in me that it was also required, a culturally expected behavior. Later, as life beat me down, I saw a harsher reality where "thank you" was used as a way of getting something, of manipulating via reciprocity.

It wasn't until I saw horrific, harmful, hurtful deeds in the world and hope and resilience reemerged that I truly understood what being grateful meant. That's when I learned how to appreciate and say "thank you" from the heart with no expectation of return. I moved through the three meanings, the three levels of thank you, as I matured.

Takeaways

Gratitude has many cousins: mindfulness, optimism, joy, reciprocity, and trust. Each has a role that is different than gratitude, but can coexist with it or support it.

Gratitude as a foundation can keep the negative aspects of these cousins (such as optimism bias and manipulative influence) in check.

Here are some additional key takeaways from this chapter:

- Gratitude and mindfulness are similar but different. While they support each other, mindfulness by itself is not action-oriented whereas gratitude is.

- Gratitude accepts the present reality and doesn't step over facts.

- Gratitude and optimism are closely related, yet can have vastly different impacts and outcomes.

- There are three meanings for "thank you": reciprocity, politeness, and gratitude.

- Thank you from a place of gratitude expects nothing in return.

Internal Reflection and Discussion

1. Take a full day and examine your use of "thank you" and how you show appreciation for others. What meaning is behind your thanks: reciprocity, politeness, or gratitude?

2. Whom do you trust and not trust, and why? For those that you do *not* trust, what about them makes you grateful?

3. What is your relationship between gratitude and trust, optimism, and happiness? Where would you rate yourself on the spectrum of each?

External Reflection and Discussion

1. What words or phrases do you, your team, or organization use that are similar to gratitude (for example: appreciation, rewards, grace)? How are they used?

2. What is the relationship between those words and phrases and gratitude?

3. Give some examples of organizational currency or business-related reciprocity that works, as well as some examples of reciprocity that does not work.

How to Play the GLAD Game

When you are grateful, fear disappears and abundance appears.
Tony Robbins

Never doubt that a small group of thoughtful, committed, citizens can change the world. Indeed, it is the only thing that ever has.
Margaret Mead

When Pollyanna's aunt sent her to her room as punishment for being late for dinner, she used "the glad game" to say how wonderful the view was from her window. It became a tool she used to find the good in everything.

A somewhat sarcastic use of the glad game comes from Monty Python's classic cult hit, *The Life of Brian*. At the end of the movie, the song "Always Look on the Bright Side of Life" is sung when no hope is left and the hero is about to be crucified and its catchy tune instructs us that, if life seems jolly rotten, we've forgotten to laugh and smile and dance and sing. It urges us to look at things in a positive light and reminds us that this is a choice we all make.

No matter how dark and dire and horrific a situation is, there is always a bright side, something to be grateful for. Gratitude is the guiding light, even if it doesn't show up until later, like it did for

James Stockdale, who became thankful for his experience as a prisoner after being released.

> *"No matter how dark the night, how bleak the circumstances, if you are alive, gratitude is a light that can bring you out of the dark."*

Elie Wiesel—a 1986 Nobel Peace winner and author of over 40 books—calls gratitude the core of humanity. *Night* is one of the hardest and most horrifying books I have ever read. Even thinking about it brings tears to my eyes.

In *Night*, Wiesel bears witness to his painful nightmare of Holocaust survival. He lost everything—his community, his family, his faith. He endured and saw others endure horrific suffering. Survival was all he was capable of and *Night* is his story that he wrote to help him understand.

In speaking of Wiesel, Robert A. Brown, the president of Boston University, said, "He did not just describe the past—although that alone would have been a profound service. Because of his erudition and his compassion, he taught us how to live in ways that overcome hate."

Part of Wiesel's healing process was to "become thankful for the small things," to be alive, and to see people living. He didn't forget the horrible memories. No, he felt a responsibility to remember them, as that was his reality, so he allowed both the horrible and the grateful to exist in him at the same time.

Wiesel believed strongly in gratitude and, in an interview with Oprah, said, "When a person does not have gratitude, something is missing in his or her humanity. A person can almost be defined by his or her attitude toward gratitude."

Putting gratitude into a work context seems almost trivial in comparison to this type of life-and-death struggle that many have endured, but it still has an effect. And what makes gratitude difficult in a work setting is the bringing together of different people, backgrounds, cultures, and levels of belief in gratitude.

Gratitude's contagious attribute can create overzealous gratitude warriors whose first question when in a difficult or challenging situation becomes: "What are you grateful for?" In some cases, this causes raised eyebrows or is ignored or ridiculed. However, if the team or culture is steeped in gratitude, asking what are we grateful for can be an amazing way to start an effective troubleshooting process.

Using an Approach of Gratitude: GLAD

If you aren't feeling gratitude or if following an approach of gratitude doesn't come naturally to you, the GLAD Tool is a great way to help you shift into gratitude. It can also be used to coach individual and with teams.

Gratitude guarantees that your outcome will be different, whether you're using it in a simple, difficult, or complex situation.

When it isn't used, we see more blaming, lack of responsibility and self-confidence. We also see more revenge and negative thinking.

The difference can be illustrated by this simple situation, which happens frequently when someone isn't given due credit for his or her idea in a meeting. Not being in a grateful mindset in this type of scenario usually results in:

- Resenting the person who spoke up about the idea you had

- Anger at the person for stealing the idea

- Anger at yourself for not speaking up

- Speaking up and sounding defensive or arrogant

- Speaking up and sounding angry or accusatorial

- You could be seen as egotistical, not a team player, or a trouble-maker (personal impact)

- The idea is shut down or not explored; your fear of speaking up causes you to hold back and the meeting could become de-railed (team impact)

Being in a grateful mindset in the same situation drastically changes these responses:

- Appreciation for the person getting the idea out so it can be used, regardless of whose idea it was initially

- Grateful for a lesson learned based on how and what the person did to get the idea heard

- Speaking up in a neutral, non-sarcastic, appreciative tone: "Thank you, what a great idea!" "I had a similar thought last week and wish I would've vocalized it more so we could've gotten started on it faster." "Great minds think alike. We are both brilliant for thinking of that!"

- Could be seen as a team player who is contributing and positive (personal impact)

- Exploration and building on the idea to its fullest (team impact)

Without gratitude, we resort to what has been done before or what we know from past experiences. For example, when a complex and long-term project has failed, it's easy to become angry, blaming, defensive, or distance yourself, causing you to remove members from the team or take legal action.

Gratitude acknowledges the hard reality and doesn't step over the failure, but rather embraces it fully by examining and understanding it so it doesn't happen again or is at least recognized more quickly. This starts internally and leads to behaviors and actions that are expansive and inclusive.

Gratitude helps you:

- Keep an open mind

- Stay calm

- Find the root cause

- Acknowledge and handle the difficult

- Discover new options

- Understand if someone is fit for a job (or not)

Acknowledging and working with a positive, engaged, and grateful approach where each person feels heard and understood contributes to rectifying the situation or, at a minimum, learning what to do differently the next time when faced with a similar issue.

In terms of business value, think about of the costs of not being grateful. If someone in a meeting steals an idea, for instance, a team member may spend hours, days, or weeks ruminating, checked out, or not engaged.

Gratitude can be applied in many business situations to create powerful results, even those that seem complex, overwhelming, or create a crisis. It allows us to see the larger context outside ourselves and to see ourselves in context of the larger world.

From a scientific point of view, gratitude moves us out of survival lockdown mode and into a more open and receptive place, a place where we can more easily problem-solve. Mindfulness achieved through meditation and other methods creates an open awareness and allows us to be truly grateful. This directs behaviors that lead to results and results are the langue of business.

Gratitude is about taking responsibility. It is a pathway to more efficient and sustainable performance improvement. It also creates more positive, collaborate, learning teams and workforces. One way to achieve it is with the GLAD Tool.

GLAD Tool

The GLAD Tool is something I use frequently with my clients to help them create a gratitude approach and GLAD is an acronym that stands for: Grateful, Lessons, Analysis, and Doing.

Grateful. What are you grateful for in this particular situation?

Lessons. What lessons have you learned? What lessons still need to be learned?

Analysis. What happened and how? What are your choices? What is the impact of the event?

Doing. Take the lessons learned and the analysis and turn them into actionable steps going forward. (Sometimes the action taken is nothing more than consciously choosing to just be grateful.)

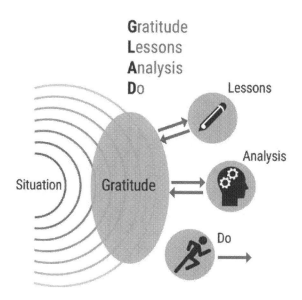

GLAD Tool for Managing a Situation

There are many business situations that are difficult and challenging and can easily bring up negative reactions of fear, anger, or indifference. Some of the most common include:

- Being fired, laid off, or removed from a position
- Being in a rude, disrespectful, nasty, and gossip-filled environment
- Having incompetent leaders, managers, and teams
- Having too much work, too little time, or feeling overwhelmed
- Having benefits or salary reduced
- Projects are delivered late or are over budget
- Projects are complex and create critical challenges

The next two charts show how this works in action. The first, shows the G (Gratitude) and the L (Lessons) of the GLAD Tool and the second takes the same situation and applies the A (Analysis) and the D (Doing).

Chart: G-Glad, L-Lessons—Fear/Anger/Indifference vs. Gratitude/Lessons		
Situation	Fear/Anger/Indifference Attitude and Thoughts	Grateful/Lesson Attitude and Thoughts
Job or Position Loss	I can't survive. They need me. I don't care.	Opportunity for a better job/position. Meet, try, or do something new. Time to focus on my dreams.
Too Much Work/Too Little Time Overwhelm, Stress	I'll lose my job or get demoted. They don't get it; jerks. Oh, well.	I have a job. I am capable. I can learn prioritization/time management skills.
Negative People: Nasty, Rude, Disrespectful, Gossips, Blamers	We can't get anything done. I'll get fired. It's their fault. I'll ignore it.	Opportunity to learn how to handle them. Empathize and get to know them better. Become clear on my boundaries.
Incompetent Person or Team	I'll never find a replacement. I can't fire someone. Some jerk put them on this team. I don't care.	I can teach them. I see what skills they are missing and know how to teach them or know someone who can. It's a reminder that not everyone has these skills. I can use my child-like mind and see as a beginner.
Benefits/Salary Reduced	I can't live on this reduced amount. They don't get it. Oh well.	Is this necessary for the business to survive? Chance to review expenses. Opportunity to exit.
Project Late/Over Budget	I'll never get ahead. It's their fault. It doesn't matter; it's not my money.	Unite the team to resolve. Chance to improve and learn. Chance to practice difficult conversations.
Difficult, Complex, Critical Issue	This is impossible. We'll never figure it out. It doesn't matter.	Expands my experience. Satisfaction in solving.

Chart: A-Analysis, D-Doing—Analysis and Doing from Fear/Anger/Indifference vs. Gratitude		
Situation	**Fear/Anger/Indifference Analysis and Doing**	**Grateful/Lesson Analysis and Doing**
Job or Position Loss	It's their fault. Yell, sue, derogate. Plot revenge. Harm organization.	Understand as much as possible about what happened. Find a better job. Leave with grace.
Too Much Work, Too Little Time Overwhelm, Stress	Sales oversells, tools inadequate, not enough people. Work harder, cut corners, quit.	Find the root cause, prioritize, put systems in place.
Negative People: Nasty, Rude, Disrespectful, Gossips, Blamers	Blame them, personalize it, stay away from them. Give negative reviews and feedback.	Empathize, be caring. Learn how to manage difficult people.
Incompetent Person or Team	Blame the person who hired or put them there. Fire or ignore them.	Figure out how the mismatch happened. Learn how to handle difficult people. Make a plan for their growth or removal in a respectful way.
Benefits/Salary Reduced	Blame the industry or your boss. Do less work.	Empathize. Find a way to be more productive and improve morale.
Project Late/Over Budget	Find out why and blame a person, team, or technology. Ignore it or keep going with a negative attitude.	Find the root cause and create a plan so it doesn't happen again.
Difficult, Complex, Critical Issue	Give up. Create a temporary solution or offer an alternative.	Consider it a puzzle; use analysis tools and solve the problem.

When operating from fear, anger, or indifference, nothing gets better. In some cases, the situation gets worse. A team that is behind schedule and blames its members creates a negative and unmotivated environment where it can take twice as long (if not more) to deliver when compared to an engaged, positive team that is working together and motivated.

The GLAD Tool is part facilitator and part coach. If you're in a face-to-face meeting, you can sometimes see the physical shift in body language and facial expression when others use it to transition from survival mode to being open and positive. When in gratitude, the face is softer with less tension around the eyes, hands unclench, and the body as a whole is in a more relaxed posture. On a conference call, you may detect a voice-tone shift as the other person begins to speak calmer and slower.

Pay attention to the questions asked and statements made as they are key to knowing when to ask others what they are grateful for. If someone is blaming, defensive, hurt, or fearful, for instance, it is *not* the time to shift to gratitude because they need to feel heard and validated before the shift can occur. Each person varies in when they shift.

Additionally, the four GLAD components can be done in any order. If you're an engineering, technical, or logical team, you'll likely want to start with the analysis first. However, a team with an already-strong culture of gratitude may start by asking what they are grateful for.

The GLAD Tool simply ensures that the situation at hand is being handled with an underlying belief of gratitude so results are more holistic, reality-based, creative, and innovative. Fear, blaming, anger, and indifference fade away as team members become more engaged, collaborative, and successful.

Coaching Others Using GLAD

Scott, a brilliant and talented technical director at a large international company, was starting to emerge as an up-and-coming leader. However, one of the biggest challenges he faced was working with the CIO (the Chief Information Officer), who had a personality very different than his own.

Scott believed that the CIO was harming his career by belittling his initiatives. I started using the GLAD Tool with him by asking what he was grateful for when it came to the CIO. His response was quick and to the point: nothing, the CIO had no value, and he was definitely not nice.

Scott went on for a while, creating a strong case for what the CIO was doing and saying that "proved" him to be worthless. During this process, Scott reiterated several times that he was positive there was nothing good in this other person.

When he was done, the first thing we did was shift to the A (Analyzing). As we reviewed a handful of their interactions, Scott made a summarizing point about each one.

For instance, one time his summarizing point was, "The CIO wanted me to leave the company." To this, I offered possible alternative stories or reasons for the CIO saying what he did. Could the CIO's response been out of fear that Scott would take *his* job? Or maybe the CIO saw Scott's talent as being wasted with the company?

By allowing Scott to be heard and taking the time necessary to analyze and dissect each point he made—offering alternative conclusions for each one—he was able to expand his viewpoint. We also clarified the facts and beliefs to identify which were real versus those he was simply telling himself, but were potentially untrue.

About 30 minutes into our session, Scott had an a-ha moment. From there, he went on to say positive things about the CIO, sharing how he was very persistent and kept at something until it was done.

Other positive qualities Scott shared about the CIO included being very giving (especially to the community), not running from conflict, and even being a great dresser, to which we both cracked up laughing.

When he thought of the CIO negatively, Scott had no idea what to do next or how to resolve their differences. He felt stuck, avoided and ignored the CIO as much as he possibly could, and even wanted to leave the company. When he was finally able to see some positive characteristics, other possibilities surfaced for improving this very important relationship.

The L (Lesson) for Scott was to check his unverified conclusions and be more open to a personality type different than his own. The D (Doing) involved finding a joint project for them to work on, while also being more vulnerable and open, and not jumping to conclusions.

Before we used the GLAD Tool, Scott was stuck and unable to move forward. After, he was grateful to the CIO for teaching him. He was also able to see how he'd made negative judgments and that the relationship was not as damaged as he'd thought.

If you're struggling with the lessons learned or in developing gratitude, if either is not feeling clear, more pondering and analysis may be required. Digging deeper into the A (Analysis) can be the most difficult part of the GLAD process. But this is also where the biggest breakthroughs tend to occur.

Additionally, it's sometimes difficult to see ourselves and our blind spots. In cases like this, working through the analysis with a trusted advisor who can give you honest feedback is an option to consider.

Coaching Yourself Using GLAD

Sometimes you need to step back and become aware of your emotional state. Are you feeling calm, open, and nonjudgmental or are you stuck in survival mode?

If you recognize that you're in survival mode (fight, flight, or freeze), your analysis will be difficult and unlikely show you all the possibilities. Shifting to mindfulness changes this.

Another technique is to distance yourself from the trigger situation. This doesn't involve denying or avoiding the emotional part of the situation, but instead labeling the emotions and being able to analyze them from a calm and mindful place. It's like walking in someone else shoes, but they are really your own!

Seven-Step Trigger Analysis

If you'd prefer a more step-by-step approach for analyzing difficult or challenging situations, there's one other technique you can use. It's called a Seven-Step Trigger Analysis and these steps can be applied in simple and complex situations alike, helping you find a workable resolution. The seven steps are:

#1—Define the Problem. Identify and clearly and concisely state the challenge or difficult situation.

#2—Identify Possible Outcomes. Do an initial pass of the potential outcomes, as well as identifying the results you want.

#3—Start with the Facts. Facts are undisputable and provable, so list as many relevant facts as possible. Questions to ask yourself include:

- Can they be proven?
- Can they be measured?
- Do contradicting facts exist?
- Are they stories or conclusions, therefore, not facts?

#4—Move to Beliefs. Identify the beliefs you have regarding the situation. Ask yourself:

- What values are supported or violated?
- What do others believe?
- What would I like to believe?
- What is the larger vision?
- What lesson does this teach?

#5—Move to Feeling. Pay attention to the emotions you're experiencing as a result of the situation. Ask:

- What am I feeling?
- What might others be feeling?
- What other feelings are there?
- What will never be felt here?

#6—Move to Analysis of Doing/Actions. Decide the actions you can potentially take to resolve the situation. To help with this, ask yourself:

- If money and time were no issue, what would I do?
- What are all of the possible actions I can take?
- What are the pros and cons of each action?
- What outcomes, results, and impact (both short and long term) will each action produce?
- When does the action need to be taken? By who? How?
- What is next?

 # 7—Validate Desired Results. Run each of the possible outcomes from step two through the analysis to see which one is most likely to provide your most desired result.

Perfectionism and Gratitude, a Tricky Coexistence

Brittany is an executive coach and perfectionist. Her goal was to become more positive and accepting as there were many situations that triggered her tumble into negative self-judgment. This would set off her perfectionism and she would then spend days (and weeks) perfecting and rearranging the areas of her life she thought responsible for the pain.

By using the analysis part of the GLAD Tool, this helped her make the shift to being more positive and letting go. Over the course of years, we analyzed the situations that set her off and came up with alternative stories and beliefs to potentially explain the situations that caused her to tumble into harsh self-judgments.

Brittany was open "trying on" these various beliefs for a day or two to validate them. For instance, if a client wasn't returning her calls or didn't hire her, instead of believing she'd done something wrong or something imperfect, she tried on an alternative belief. Maybe the client decided not to hire anyone, or perhaps the client had a family tragedy or the organization cut funding?

Once an alternative story was created that she felt comfortable with, Brittany became grateful for the opportunity to learn. But this learning wasn't possible until negative self-judgment was out of the picture.

A majority of the time, when she *did* finally find out the facts, Brittany realized that it wasn't about her. Other times, she never discovered the facts at all. In those cases, she chose to learn and just let go of the stories altogether. (The joke we had was that the world did *not* revolve around her and how perfect she was.)

Eventually, the lesson Brittany learned was that she was judging herself and beating herself up for not doing things the right way, kicking off her perfectionism. I knew the process had worked effectively for her when her largest and most financially lucrative client let her go and, within days, she was truly grateful and had moved on to bigger and better work. Before her shift to gratitude, she would've spent months (if not years) judging herself and perfecting every detail of her business.

Admittedly, some situations still bother her, but now Brittany knows what to do to catch her negative thoughts and shift to gratitude. As a result, self-judgment no longer consumes her. It has taken years, but being mindful and grateful has now become a natural way of being for Brittany. This has made her life easier and her business more lucrative.

That, in a nutshell, is the GLAD Tool. Take a difficult situation and work it until you can shift and approach it from a place of being grateful. Learn from it, analyze it, and figure out what actions are possible to move forward from a place of gratitude.

The GLAD Tool acknowledges that it isn't easy to always be grateful, but it does help you switch to gratitude faster so you can reap the benefits. Using it for challenging situations—like the ones highlighted in the GLAD charts and in Scott and Brittany's stories— helps you get unstuck and create new possible avenues for moving forward.

As Monty Python says, "If all else fails, look on the bright side, you are not being crucified. You are alive."

Takeaways

Whether the situation is simple, difficult, or complex, gratitude guarantees different outcomes with more and better options and actions.

When gratitude is *not* used, there is more blaming, lack of responsibility, and lower self-confidence. You also see more anger, fear, indifference, and revengeful and negative thinking.

The GLAD Tool provides a path to gratitude and is a way to switch to a state of gratitude more quickly.

Here are some of the additional key takeaways from this chapter:

- The GLAD approach stands for Gratitude, Lessons, Analysis, and Doing.

- The GLAD Tool shifts individuals and teams to gratitude. It's a process that leads to the question: what am I grateful for?

- The A (Analysis) is based on data and facts and many organizations are already using similar processes, so it's a good place to start.

- Being in survival mode makes analysis very difficult, whereas mindfulness brings you to a state of calm and nonjudgmental openness.

- The Seven-Step Analysis helps you analyze situations at an even deeper level, providing more possibilities and choices for moving forward and taking action. It's not a way to ignore what is happening, but rather to step back from the emotions and do a fact-based analysis.

- Using the GLAD Tool is not about achieving perfection as perfectionism and gratitude have a hard time co-existing.

Internal Reflection and Discussion

1. Take a challenging situation you currently face and use the Seven-Step Analysis to separate fact from your beliefs and feelings. Consider the alternative beliefs and feelings someone else might have in this same situation. (Going through this process may take you a few days or weeks, depending on how big the challenge is. So, give yourself adequate time.)

2. Write down the lesson learned from this situation as though you were looking back on it years from now.

3. What might you do about this situation when operating from a place of gratitude?

External Reflection and Discussion

Imagine that a high-risk event has occurred—maybe even one that is already listed in your business continuity or risk plan—and role play the meeting held afterward using the GLAD Tool.

(Sample scenarios: your IT center is down for three to five days, your key lead has to be away from work during a critical delivery, or a disaster like a hurricane or wildfire shuts down your site.)

1. Compare a troubleshooting process or tool that you currently use to the GLAD Tool. (If you don't have a process you follow or tool you typically use, Google "post project lessons learned" or simply ask and answer the question "why?" five times.)

2. In a meeting, what signs exist that people aren't operating from a place of gratitude? What do they say? How do they say it? What do they do?

3. Pick one challenging issue or something your team is stuck on and use the GLAD Tool.

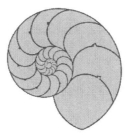

PART 4
D IS FOR DOING

For gratitude to take hold and flourish in ourselves and our organizations, we must first understand the internal and external obstacles that prevent it. We must then act if we want to increase our own gratitude muscle and build cultures of gratitude.

Every gratitude building plan is unique and works best if it's customized. Therefore, you need to know where you are now by measuring the extent of your current individual and team gratitude practices.

Part 4 offers a Personal Gratitude Assessment to help with this. By understanding the five traits that compromise a holistic gratitude practice, you can use this information to create an individualized, effective gratitude plan for you and your team. Part 4 also addresses some of the common challenges with gratitude.

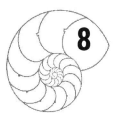

Assessing Gratitude

I'm not afraid to throw it (gratitude) out there. People can't believe
I'm so forward with it, and it's not a canned speech. It's genuine.

Sonia Gauthier, Settlement Agent for Accurate Title

Businesses run based on predicted outcomes. How many people will we hire? How will our stock perform this quarter? How many units will we ship? How much money will we spend?

The project management profession predicts these future outcomes with a tool called the Iron Triangle (also called the Triple Constraint). This triangle uses three key components to make these predictions:

1. How much it will cost? (budget)

2. How long it will take? (schedule)

3. What will it be? (scope, features, quality)

A project manager gets as specific as possible about the relationship between each of these three components then uses the information provided to create and manage a plan.

Though business would be much easier if we could predict and control the future—which businesses desperately want to be able to do--gratitude promises none of this.

Gratitude is not about control. Instead, it is the rich soil that organizations grow and thrive in, benefiting them by connecting and engaging people. Gratitude leads to increased productivity which leads to improving the bottom line. It is the cultural lubricant that enables the Iron Triangle to operate effortlessly, with less friction.

However, because it is intangible and underlying, how do we really know if we are improving on building our gratitude? Further, how do we know if we have high performers who are underappreciated and, therefore, not performing their best?

Are people too nice, causing them to not set appropriate boundaries for working on what's important? Are there people who are negative and self-important, causing teams to implode? *How do we know?*

Unfortunately, we cannot know until we are open to seeing each other's vulnerabilities and more trusting of ourselves and others. Gratitude creates a culture and environment that is productive, innovative, and open to discussions that have a chance of producing amazing results. But it also doesn't promise to solve all woes.

The Gratitude Assessment is one way for individuals, teams, and businesses to engage in more gratitude. From it comes tangible measurements of the intangible gratitude. Taking these measurements, we can then create a plan to improve our gratitude practices as, without it, you'll never really know what you and your organization are capable of. You'll never realize what is missing.

Attributes That Measure Gratitude

In God we trust, all others must bring data.

Edward Deming

Before honing the GLAD Tool, I was a bit too zealous and used to start sessions by asking, "What are you grateful for?" People's responses generally fell into one of these four categories:

1. *Crazy. Did you hear what I said?* (Did I not just listen to how bad, horrible, awful, or difficult their situation was?)

2. *Ignored.* No response whatsoever. They silently dismissed my question completely, often with raised eyebrows.

3. *Loss.* They saw my gratitude response as a lack of empathy for where they were emotionally, causing them to feel hurt and as if they were losing a connection or relationship.

4. *Angry. How could you ask such a thing?* (Was I just trying to pick a fight? Because, clearly, gratitude doesn't apply here.)

A few times, I followed up and asked what was going through their minds when I asked about being grateful. One person responded, "It was rude you didn't hear me." She didn't want to be grateful; she was upset. So, I asked what I could've done to help move her to a place of gratitude. Her answer? Nothing.

Rarely does asking the gratitude question shift someone who isn't in a positive place. Sometimes people aren't ready and don't want to shift to gratitude. Other times, using the GLAD Tool helps move them to gratitude or at least right up to the precipice of being grateful.

Sometime people want to be grateful but don't know how. Just saying you are grateful or that you should be grateful doesn't always create feelings of gratitude.

Remember in the case of coaching Scott, it took about 30 minutes before he was able to make the shift. Being in there with him—being beside him, connecting with him, and showing care and empathy—provided the support necessary for shifting to a positive mindset.

How do you know if you're successfully building a culture and practice of gratitude? How do you take something intangible like gratitude and measure it so it *is* tangible? The trick is to find attributes you can measure and then create a ruler to take the needed measurements.

But measurement is only the first step as the next is to self-assess. Self-assessing helps actually engage you in gratitude versus just taking an assessment that tells you how grateful you are.

The numbers a person or team assigns to their own gratitude measurements almost don't matter because they are relative to each individual self-assessment. The point is: there is always a next step or next place to improve.

After taking the Personal Gratitude Assessment, a plan for gratitude improvement must be created. Each plan is unique and will likely take several iterations before becoming optimal. These adjustments are based on whether you see or not as an effective gratitude practice adapts to where you are now as well as where you want to be in the future.

Certain factors can affect how this change and adaptation occur. Sometimes, they can force you to "double down" on your gratitude practice in an effort to achieve higher results. These include:

- Divisive political environments
- Disasters (natural or man-made)
- Personal tragedies

- Job loss or reorganization

- Company acquisitions

- Acquisition or loss of an important client

When these types of situations occur, ramping up your gratitude practice and/or shifting how you practice may be required. To recap: the process to improve gratitude follows these four steps:

1. *Measure gratitude.* Use the Gratitude Assessment individually, as a team, or as an organization. Complete a Gratitude Circle Inventory.

2. *Create a plan.* Creating a plan for teams and organizations may involve reviewing and integrating elements of gratitude into people, technology, and processes. What training is needed? What is the desired culture?

3. **Practice.** Use the Three-Step Gratitude Process to shift to gratitude with the GLAD Tool.

4. *Reassess and revise.* Revisit your gratitude plan every 30 days, 6 months, and/or 1 year, revising it as needed.

Five Gratitude Assessment Attributes

After reviewing hundreds of research studies on gratitude from all over the world, I've discovered that the five attributes most commonly used to measure gratitude are:

1. Intensity

2. Frequency

3. Breadth

4. Environment or context

5. Gratitude-based behaviors and habits

In the image on the following page, these attributes are represented in an interlocked, integrated circle because they support and build off each other. For instance, the deeper you feel gratitude (intensity), the more often you feel it (frequency), the more things you are grateful for (breadth), or the more your environment supports it, the more it shows up in your behaviors.

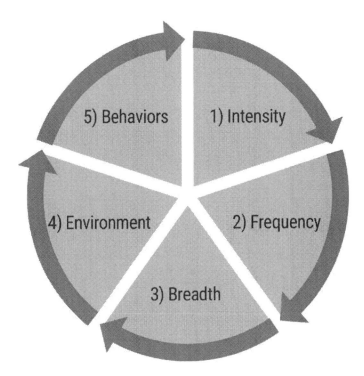

Attribute #1—Intensity

How capable are you of feeling gratitude on a deeper, more intense level? Expressions such as "my heart is overflowing" and "my heart is about to burst" are deeply intense feelings of gratitude. The other end of the spectrum is not experiencing gratitude at all or being neutral, while the middle of the road is a mere, mildly intense feeling of gratitude.

The deepest, most intense feeling of joy, happiness, and gratitude I've ever experienced is the birth of my sons. For days after, the world was perfect and joyous. Since practicing and building my gratitude muscle, I now experience that same level of intensity a few times a month. Some people experience it daily. Sadly, others have never experienced it at all.

Looking at the spectrum of options on a gratitude scale, what is the most intense level of gratitude *you've* experienced?

• It's pretty neutral, I've never really experienced gratitude.
• I've felt a slight appreciation for things.
• I've felt happy and grateful from time to time.
• I've felt extremely grateful before.
• I have experienced deep and intense gratitude.

Attribute #2—Frequency

During the course of an average day, how often do you feel grateful? Do you have morning or nighttime gratitude habits or rituals in place to remind you to be grateful?

Those who were interviewed for this book because I identified them as being grateful reported that they were grateful 75 to 95 percent of the day. What percentage of your day are *you* feeling grateful?

Attribute #3—Breadth

How many different things are you grateful for? Your brain, your body? Your personality? Your health?

Moving out into your environment, are you grateful for your chair? The desk? The room? The items in the room? Your office?

What about the people closest to you, whether currently alive or not? Are you grateful for your neighborhood, your community, your town, your state, or your country?

Be as concrete and as abstract as you like as you consider the breadth of your gratitude. After looking at your list, how many things are *you* grateful for?

- There are very few things I'm grateful for.
- There are some things I'm grateful for.
- There are a lot of things I'm grateful for.
- I am grateful for most everything.
- I can find something to be grateful for in everything.

If you can find something to be grateful for even in the people, ideas, or things that you dislike, you have a high level of gratitude breadth.

Attribute #4—Environment

When considering the people and places you interact with daily, are they filled with gratitude or are you the lone person being grateful?

If you've practiced gratitude a good portion of your life and have primarily worked in environments that support it, you will naturally attract people and places that share a similar view. On the other hand, if the environment and people around you don't support gratitude, it's more difficult to stay grateful.

Granted, you don't choose your biological family and you may not be able to choose your neighbors either, but you *can* limit how much you interact with these individuals if they decide to not be grateful.

Watching a TV channel that constantly streams bad news makes it difficult to stay grateful as well, as does having a disorganized or dirty office.

During the course of any given day, how much does *your* environment and the people you interact with support and reinforce your ability to live a life of gratitude? (Your environment includes all the places you frequent like your office, your car, your home, your community.)

- There is no gratitude in my environment.
- There is limited gratitude in my environment.
- There is a fair amount of gratitude in my environment.
- There is a lot of gratitude in my environment.
- My environment is filled with gratitude and things I'm grateful for.

Attribute #5—Social Behaviors and Habits

How many behaviors and daily habits do you have that promote, support, and reinforce gratitude?

Are you like Sonia, who isn't afraid to throw lots of gratitude and appreciation out during almost all of her conversations (even difficult ones), so others feel welcome and appreciated? Maybe you're like Susan, who writes handwritten thank-you letters daily to people she appreciates or Mike, who wrote over 230 letters of appreciation to work colleagues in less than a year?

These are extreme examples, but even something as simple as saying "thank you" when you appreciate something, using positive words, setting boundaries in a positive way, or not complaining, gossiping, or judging can help you get (and stay) in gratitude.

When interacting with others, how often does gratitude appear in *your* behaviors?

- I don't appreciate or acknowledge others.
- I show minimal levels of gratitude.
- I appreciate and acknowledge others on a regular basis; I regularly use positive words and phrases.

- Occasionally, I go above and beyond to recognize and appreciate others.

- Every day I strive to go above and beyond with gratitude; I go out of my way to show appreciation for others.

Your initial responses to this assessment are called your baseline or starting point. From there, you are able to create a plan that addresses the areas that need the most work or that you are most motivated to improve.

Down the road, measure again and compare the results against your baseline to see how you're doing. Some people find it helpful to measure daily, others weekly, and still others, once a year. Generally speaking, it takes about a month to see an improvement, sometimes longer.

One word of caution: the numbers are only as good as you define and align them to your desired outcomes. In other words, they are only accurate if you are honest and set clear goals.

Since they're only numbers, you can make them say anything you want. It is your interpretation and translation that determines what the intensity of a 3 in gratitude might mean, for instance.

For this reason, consistency is required when defining what the numbers actually mean. And if the definitions you've created aren't working, don't be afraid to redefine them.

To help with this process, you can use the Personal Gratitude Assessment Worksheet on the following page.

Personal Gratitude Assessment Worksheet			
Attribute	**Rating (1 to 5)**	**Today**	**6 Mo.**
Intensity What's the most intense level of gratitude you feel?	1 = Neutral 2 = Slight Appreciation 3 = Grateful 4 = Very Grateful 5 = Deep and Intense		
Frequency What percentage of your day do you feel grateful?	1 = 0–20% 2 = 21–40% 3 = 41–60% 4 = 61–80% 5 = 81–100%		
Breadth How many things are you grateful for? Include things, people, ideas, technology, process, everything!	1 = None 2 = 1–20 3 = 21–50 4 = 51 to hundreds 5 = Everything		
Environment How well does your daily environment support gratitude? (Office, home, work, vehicle, colleagues, family, friends, technology)	1 = Not at all 2 = Some 3 = About half 4 = Almost all are supportive 5 = All are supportive		
Behaviors When interacting with others daily, how grateful are your behaviors? Do you say "thank you" and speak in positive terms?	1 = No appreciation of others 2 = Minimal appreciation 3 = Regularly appreciate 4 = Go out of my way to show appreciation 5 = Go above and beyond daily		

For decades, I've taught communication workshops on how to have difficult conversations, give feedback, and influence others. Many times, the question comes up that, despite having so many tips and techniques available, how come they either (1) aren't all used or (2) don't work?

The simple answer is, when both people involved have trust and gratitude, it makes having tough conversations, giving critical feedback, and influencing less difficult (not necessarily easy, just not as hard) and has a better chance of success.

Ironically, the techniques and tips used become less important when gratitude is utilized in a trusting environment. Trust and gratitude combined allow for a great deal of forgiveness, openness, and motivation for making things work out.

When the tips and techniques tend to become more important is when the number of people involved increases. This is mainly because this is also when trust and gratitude typically dissipate.

For example, a manager with a heavy accent that is at times difficult to understand is much less likely to destroy trust when in a one-to-one conversation with a trusted peer by saying something inappropriate or incorrect as long as he or she is coming from a place of gratitude.

However, that same manager having a difficult conversation with a team without building a trusting environment first would be wise to apply communication tips and techniques and practice clear and concise communication to avoid any potential issues.

The Gratitude Circle Inventory

It's important to create triggers in your work and
in your life to remember to focus on gratitude.

Marshall Goldsmith

The Gratitude Circle Inventory is a visual tool designed to help you count the breadth of things you are grateful for in both your personal and professional life. It can be used independently or in combination with the Gratitude Assessment. The nautilus shaped circle starts with you at the center and each chamber expands outwardly to the larger world. When using it, you assign a label to each chamber and write down or count how many things you are grateful for and write the number in that chamber.

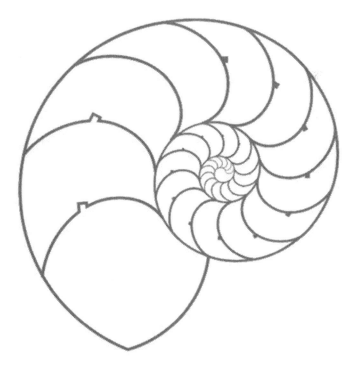

For example, one of the inner chambers I call "physical me." In it, I gave myself a 5 for my health, mind, body, hair, and eyes. If you come across something you are ungrateful for in that chamber, gently—and without judgment—write down and count those negatives as well. Again, for me, my negatives for physical me is -2 (for my weight and allergies).

Now, move to the next chamber and label it with your next category and do the same. When conducting a Personal Gratitude Circle Inventory, suggested categories are:

- *Me.* Heart, values, beliefs, vision

- *Health.* Physical well-being, nutrition, exercise

- *Personal.* Spiritual, learning, well-being, mental health

- *Finances.* Income, expenses, savings

- *Fun/Recreation.* Sports, games, crafts, volunteer work, hobbies, vacations

- *Family.* Those you see every day, sometimes close friends

- *Friends.* Extended family or community

- *Career/Job.* The career you are in

- *Physical Environment.* Home, vehicle, office, yard, neighborhood

List and/or tally your positives and negatives. For example, my office would have a +8 because I'm grateful for my books, laptop, plants, pictures, whiteboard, couch, pens, and CD player. It also has a -1 for my printer, which I'm not so grateful for.

Repeat this same process, expanding outward until you exhaust all chambers and are at the universe. Date it with today's date because the rating is for this moment in time, not what it was yesterday or what you hope it will be tomorrow.

When doing the Gratitude Circle Inventory for business, again, start with you at the center. Except, this time, use business-related categories such as Me, Team, Organization, Industry, and Business Climate. When creating a Business Gratitude Circle Inventory, my suggested labels are:

- *Sales.* Skills, closing rate, pipeline, contracts

- *Marketing.* Awareness, business cards, website, social media, advertisements, networking

- *Expert.* Best in class, mastering your craft

- *Organization/Teams.* Your teams, support, cross-functional teams

- *Business Operations.* Equipment, accounting, taxes, offices, processes, regulations, legal, IT infrastructure

- *Vision, Goals, Strategy.* Direction, plans, values, culture

- *Product or Service Offerings.* Things sold or given away, end results

- *Customers.* Clients (past, current, and future), customer service

For each, list and tally what you are grateful for (the positives) as well as the things you're not so grateful for (the negatives). Repeat the process, labeling the categories and listing and/or counting the positives and negatives in each one as you expand outward until you reach the business economy universe.

Gratitude Circle Suggestions

You can start in any section of the gratitude circle you'd like. If you'd prefer, begin with the whole world (the outer chambers) and work inward toward you. Or start in the middle. Do what makes the most sense to you.

Additionally, some sections might not make sense or be clear if you have nothing to enter. Conversely, other things may not fit in any particular section. For these, you may want to combine them in a category labeled "miscellaneous."

This exercise is similar to post-project analysis exercises in which teams are asked what went well and what could be improved. Instead, with the Gratitude Circle, the focus is on gratitude as you're asking what you are grateful (and not so grateful) for.

Takeaways

Gratitude is intangible, so we must find a way to make it tangible and real. Measuring gratitude using the five attributes in the Gratitude Assessment paves the way for creating a baseline, whereas the Gratitude Circle Inventory is a visual tool we can use to count the breadth of things we are grateful for.

Other key takeaways from this chapter include:

- The Gratitude Assessment uses five attributes (intensity, frequency, breadth, context, and behaviors) to measure our gratitude.

- The Gratitude Inventory Circle is one way to visually measure the breadth of things we are grateful for.

Internal Reflection and Discussion

1. Take the Gratitude Assessment, giving yourself a few days to think about your answers (or to ask others you trust how they see you). Did any of your answers (or the feedback from others) surprise you or make you more conscious of gratitude?

2. Complete a Gratitude Inventory, nonjudgmentally noting what you're not grateful for as well. What do you think of the results? Did doing the inventory change anything?

3. Based on your assessment and inventory, what areas of gratitude could you focus on that would most benefit you right now?

External Reflection and Discussion

1. What intangible things (like culture, values, or beliefs) are important to your team and organization today? How might they be measured?

2. Take the Gratitude Assessment with your team. Discuss and define what each of the five attributes means before assigning them a number.

3. Analyze the team's results. What is the impact and what are the benefits of these attributes? Next, brainstorm ideas for moving your team to the next level in each of the attributes.

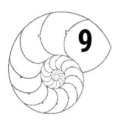

Engage with a Gratitude Plan

I have tried 99 times and failed, but on the 100th time came success.

Albert Einstein

As with any skill, you must practice to get better. Part of practicing is sometimes experiencing failure. Take Michael Jordan. He missed 9,000 shots, lost 300 games, and 26 times, he missed the game-winning shot. But look at all he accomplished because he kept going!

When I started my gratitude practice, I wrote down what I was grateful for every morning. Early on in my practice, on the more difficult days, I was grateful to be alive or for my family. Now, what I'm grateful for daily is more nuanced.

It took about two years of practicing gratitude before I saw the goodness and was grateful for negative situations in my life. Fifteen years later, I am still practicing daily, adapting and changing my practice based on my interests, newly discovered blind spots, or desired personal changes I want to make.

Practice is repetitive. It creates behaviors and habits that eventually become so ingrained that you're not aware or cannot see them. The more I practice, the more gratitude has become part of my work

with individuals, teams, and organizations. The stronger my gratitude muscle grows, the more unconscious incorporating it into my
life and work has become.

The only thing that matters when deciding how you're going to
practice gratitude is that the method you choose is effective—that it
works. It's both an art and a science to figure out what type of practice provides the best results for you as an individual, as well as for
your entire team.

But starting is also more important than figuring out the perfect
way to practice. You can (and should) adapt and change as you go.
All that matters is that your practice is consistent, which requires discipline and motivation.

At times, practice can be uncomfortable. Yet, the best muscle-
building exercises push and challenge us to reach the next level, so
we are sore the next day.

Committing to the practice for 30 days is generally enough to
make it a habit strong enough to occur without thought. Getting clear
on your motivation, being accountable, being consistent, and having
social support all aid in the building of an effective gratitude habit.

Setting Goals for a Gratitude Plan

A plan that includes a daily gratitude practice is a roadmap that
can be used for reaching your goals. That said, there are two major
things to consider before creating your own individualized plan.
First, what is your goal for gratitude?

If your plan doesn't include a goal, it becomes unclear where
you'll end up. Or, as Abraham Lincoln said, "A goal properly set is
halfway reached."

Here are some sample personal gratitude goals to consider:

• Increase my gratitude muscle

- Improve my gratitude intensity from a 3 to 5

- To be in gratitude 85 percent of the day instead of 50 percent, which is where I am now

- To be able to see and truly be grateful for the people and things in my life

- To improve my gratitude behaviors and develop a weekly practice of acknowledging others

If your gratitude goal is for a team, your goal or goals may look something like this:

- Regularly recognize positive behaviors (like working overtime).

- At every team meeting, ask what went well and what needs improvement.

- Develop and enforce ground rules that are respectful to everyone.

- Keep everyone accountable to each other.

- Show appreciation for other teams, clients, and industry pundits.

For organizations, your gratitude goals may look different yet:

- Improve employee engagement, getting it to 85 percent and ensuring it stays there by measuring it annually.

- Create processes that are clear, easy to understand, and support individuals as well as the organization

- Handle difficult and challenging situations in a fair and transparent way.

- Ensure easy-to-use rewards programs are clear and in place.

- Incorporate rewards and recognition in performance reviews in a fair and timely way.

- Train 75 percent of the employees in collaboration, teams, and trust building.

- Ensure senior executives identify and take gratitude-related actions.

- Develop regular appreciation practices and processes at all levels of the organization.

The second major consideration before creating a plan is the motivation behind setting a gratitude goal, or the benefit it will offer. This is also known as the *why*. *Why* are you willing to invest the time and energy into making this goal a reality?

For my hockey-playing son, the one who rewired his eyes to stay open when the puck came at him, he was motivated to play in the NHL. For me, my initial motivation was to heal and not hurt anymore, and instead, to see life as beautiful. Today I'm motivated because I've seen the power of gratitude for myself and my business.

Some individuals who practice gratitude don't feel they have a choice, that the opposite environment—the one they're currently in—is simply not acceptable. Senior executives may choose to embrace happiness and gratitude as a culture because they've seen or been part of negative, harmful organizations and are committed to creating positive and productive workplaces instead.

It's important for you as an individual, a team, and an organization to find the motivation behind why you are building your gratitude muscle. When you make your *why* visible, motivation sparks your goal to life—even when the process feels difficult and gratitude seems like the least important thing.

Here are a few ways both individuals and teams have kept their gratitude practice going strong:

- Assign a label or meme (Gratitude Seeker, Radical Gratitude Warrior, Conscious Cocreator of a Grateful World, Peace Warrior, Attitude of Gratitude) to reinforce and remind you why you are making these changes.

- Create a visual or physical reminder (like a business logo, vision, or values) of the importance of gratitude. One person who took one of my workshops reported that she keeps five small pebbles in her pockets every day to reminder herself of the five people in her life she is grateful for due to the impact they've had.

- Publicly commit to a plan and goal, ask someone to keep you accountable, and create a physical reminder. Pick a date six months or a year into the future and schedule a meeting to review your gratitude assessment and update your goals.

Creating Your Personal Gratitude Plan

Using gratitude in difficult situations is an approach that is easy to understand, hard to apply, but powerful when used. The more you practice, the greater the amount of time you will spend being in gratitude. The more you are grateful, the more unconsciously and naturally you will take gratitude as an approach.

How do you know whether your gratitude practice is working? When difficult situations arise and your shift to gratitude occurs faster, your practice is providing results. The quicker the shift, the stronger your gratitude muscle has become.

John knew his gratitude muscle was stronger when a customer lashed out at him in front of his team and, instead of his typical behavior of yelling in return, he unconsciously shifted to gratitude and calmly handled the situation. Afterward, he noted that he was grateful that his customers cared enough to let his company know where it was falling short, rather than just disappearing.

As you practice and experience gratitude, it begins to seep unconsciously into the underlying fabric of your life and organizations. Transformations become easier and more possibilities become available. Here is a sample Personal Gratitude Plan:

Sample Gratitude Plan: Personal	
The goal of my gratitude practice (my motivation) is:	Areas I want to focus on include:
My challenges will be:	My strengths are:
I learn best when:	Ideas I'll try include:
Action/Practice	*Measuring Results*
Daily, I will:	I will review this next and update it in: (30 days? 6 months? 1 year?)
Weekly, I will:	
Monthly, I will:	This is how I will know I've improved:
Trainings:	

About the Personal Plan

A long, complicated plan is hard to understand and follow. Therefore, from my experience, a one-page (or even shorter) plan usually works best, simply because you are more likely to remember it and refer to it more often.

The best time to create your personal gratitude plan is after completing the Gratitude Assessment and Gratitude Circle Inventory. Answering the internal and external reflection questions at the end of the previous chapters will also help.

The two most important questions to always keep in the forefront of your mind are: (1) What are the goals of my personal gratitude practice? and (2) What is the motivation for building my gratitude muscle?

Creating the most effective gratitude plan possible requires that you follow four steps. They are:

1. **Pick a focus area for your practice.** If this is the first time you are creating a conscious practice, a general focus of improving gratitude is sufficient. However, as you hone your gratitude skills, getting more specific is often helpful. (For example, my focus areas are: expanding my breadth of gratitude and externally visible gratitude behaviors.) The more realistic your plan, the more likely you are to succeed. Be honest about your strengths and challenges upfront to make it more realistic.

2. **Consider how you learn best.** What is your personality type and learning style? If you're extroverted and love social media, for instance, use this to learn and keep you accountable. If you like researching and reading, use that instead. And if you are a visual learner, consider adding a visual component to your plan by using pictures or an image-based social media platform like

Instagram or Pinterest, for example. Do you like metaphors, tactile activities, or music? Incorporate those elements into your plan.

3. **Brainstorm ideas you're willing to try.** We'll go over this in greater detail in chapter 11, which is also where you'll find a list of suggestions used by others.

4. **Decide the daily, weekly, and monthly actions you are committed to practicing when building your gratitude muscle.** When you've completed this part of the plan, reflect on it to ensure that it will get you to your desired gratitude goals.

Along the way, you may discover some new and interesting ideas or insights that are worth spending time with. Or, you may find that you get caught up in life's drama.

These types of situations and events should motivate you to review the goals you've set and determine what is most important in relation to the other things going on. Forgiving yourself and learning and adapting as you go is, sometimes, the best you can do.

Teams wanting to improve and increase gratitude (and become higher performing in the process) have many options. Holding structured, facilitated discussions on the topics included in the Team Gratitude Plan and agreeing on the desired outcomes are the first steps. The more specific and clear the team can speak to its overall goals, the better. Here's a sample Team Gratitude Plan:

Sample Gratitude Plan: Team

Our team gratitude goal and desired outcomes include:	Areas we need to focus on are:
The things that will support and/or strengthen this goal include: (processes, technology, ground rules)	Challenges outside the team's control that may get in the way of the goal are:

Actions to take	*Results*
Trainings:	This is when we will review and update our goals:
Communications (text, email, presentations):	
Processes (ground rules, reporting):	
Meetings:	

If the team already has a project plan or operating agreement, gratitude can be added as a component. For instance, I've seen project managers add requirements that are more team-culture and behavior-oriented, such as:

- The team must strive to improve at each meeting.

- The team must publicly acknowledge their successes.

- Team members must be allowed to ask for help and be supported.

When taking actionable steps to achieve these types of goals, teams typically choose to focus on areas of weakness. Depending on the team, this could be something as simple and specific as being on time or no multitasking while in team meetings. Or it could involve more complex goals of building trust and respect, or taking more risks.

Either way, a team operates within the context of a larger organization or program, so it's important to recognize what is and what is not within the team's control. It's also a good idea to ensure that a team's goals support the larger organizational goals or vision (or at least doesn't contradict them).

Cross-functional, cross-cultural, and virtual teams, and people who are on many teams, all have special challenges in how they apply gratitude. But they also have strengths, some of which include: having more experience, having a greater knowledge base, having already worked together, and access to more resources and tools.

Face-to-face meetings and other virtual communication tools are also helpful when building a team's gratitude. Brainstorming ways to improve the team's positivity and gratitude can be a meeting in and of itself.

There are many wonderful techniques and models effective in building team gratitude. For example, in *Winning the Brain Game: Fixing the Seven Fatal Flaws of Thinking*, author Matthew E. May offers some excellent suggestions on how to break out of the flaws of everyday thinking. This is important because everyday thinking gets bogged down by our desire to be perfect, over planning, being critical, over thinking, mental rigidity, jumping to action too fast, and sometimes throwing out the best ideas.

Becoming aware of which thinking flaw you and/or your team might be guilty of is the first step. May then offers exercises to overcome each type of flaw. Some of his suggestions include: self-distancing (as we discussed in step 2 of the Gratitude Shift Process), bringing in an outside opinion, fresh starts to a problem, identifying problem boundaries and going over them, and reframing the problem. He's used these insights and fixes with teams like the L.A. Bomb Squad to infuse creative thinking into their processes.

Six Thinking Hats by Edward De Bono is another approach to consider when brainstorming. In this book, De Bono encourages us to look at things six different ways using the analogy of hats. The six hats he references are those related to managing, information, emotions, logic, optimism, and creativity. This proactively forces us to think in a way we might not naturally.

Stephen Shapiro also offers a book chock-full of ideas for developing strategy and fresh thinking titled *Best Practices are Stupid: 40 Ways to Out Innovate the Competition*. You can randomly select any one of his 40 ways to develop fresh thinking and use it for the basis of a brainstorming session. For example, tip 37 is to "Stand in Someone Else's Shoe." In other words, brainstorm by pretending to be someone else and considering what you think they might say.

Once you're done brainstorming, select the actions that you as a team are willing to commit to trying. Because gratitude is behavior based, one of the most successful actions I've seen involves the use of ground rules, such as those centered around inclusion, ensuring that everyone's voice is heard.

Setting ground rules creates norms. It is also a way to show respect for all team members and allows for the proper handling of conflict. This sounds easy, but can also be very difficult to implement in the moment and to adjust for each person and team.

Once you have agreed to a set of actions and structures, check back to ensure that they will actually help you achieve your desired gratitude goals. Finally, like any successful plan, it will require regularly adaptation, revising it with your updated views and visions for the future.

The payoff is powerful for teams that embrace gratitude. It may not seem obvious at first, but when difficult problems are solved with ease, creativity, and without regret, you'll know that you've made gratitude an unconscious approach and way of being.

Complementary Skills

There are many other learnable skills that can be used to help strengthen your gratitude. When part of a gratitude plan and practice, these skills enhance and support an environment of trust, respect, and gratitude.

A few to consider are:

- Mindfulness (gratitude's closest cousin)
- Happiness, trust, and positivity (its other cousins)
- Self-awareness, identifying triggers that take you out of being grateful as well as those that put you into a state of gratitude
- Giving and receiving compliments, appreciation, and gratitude-based gifts
- Empathy, the caring and appreciation of others
- Boundaries, setting limits and expectations or saying no

- Communication to support and move others into gratitude, which includes adapting and listening

- Collaboration, team building, and leadership (skills that support working with others)

- Facilitation, an art and science that brings out the wisdom of teams

- Coaching or guiding another person to achieve his or her goals

When you review this list, think about the goals of your gratitude practice and which of these skills might enhance them. Each one is an entire area of study that can take a lifetime to master. Or maybe you're already teaching these skills to others?

Many of these skills also overlap. For example, coaching involves the use of effective communication skills of both listening *and* asking powerful questions.

In the reference section at the end of this book, I've included some resources that can be used for these additional areas. Just keep in mind that these skills require more than book learning; they must be applied and experienced.

Other options include taking a communication class to learn more about self-awareness and triggers, or working with a coach to zoom in and focus on your specific triggers and figure out how to best handle them. Empathy is another skill typically taught in emotional intelligence or coaching workshops.

One of the most important skills for a leader is communication, especially the skill of listening, and one of my favorite books on this topic is *Conversational Intelligence: How Great Leaders Build Trust and Get Extraordinary Results* by Judith E. Glaser. In it, Glaser talks about how shifting the brain into a positive place helps you identify conversations that aren't allowing all potential possibilities.

The Five Dysfunctions of a Team by Patrick M. Lencioni is another great book which focuses on collaboration and team building to enhance trust as a starting point. Facilitation, appreciative inquiry, World Café methodology, and the coaching circle techniques are all complementary to gratitude.

Coaching, a $1 billion per year industry, is about reaching our fullest potential as humans. How do we know when we've reached this level of potential? We don't. All we know is that we are grateful for where we are now and where we used to be. From that mindset, we can continue on the journey, open to all possibilities.

Takeaways

Once you have an assessment and inventory, the next step is creating a plan—one for you and one for your team. Having goals and understanding why you've chosen them sets the stage for that plan, which may either be entirely new or simply an existing plan that incorporates gratitude as a component.

Either way, this plan is a starting point for beginning or improving your gratitude practice. It needs to be revised regularly to ensure that it adapts to your internal and external changes, as well as reviewing it to determine what does and does not work.

Other key takeaways of this chapter include:

- A gratitude practice is easy to start, but requires discipline and a plan to ensure constant care and feeding.

- Finding the right practice and plan for you, your team, and organization is an art and a science, making it something that needs monitoring and review.

- Give your gratitude practice a label, metaphor, logo, or other reminder to keep it in the forefront of your mind.

- Include other skills in the plan, such as mindfulness, coaching, facilitation, and setting limits, so they can be learned and developed as well.

Internal Reflection and Discussion

1. What are the goals of your personal gratitude plan? How do they support other goals you have in your life (or don't they)? What is the overlap?

2. In the past, when you've successfully made a change or improvement, what were the conditions and environment? How can you replicate that for your gratitude plan and practice?

3. How realistic is your plan? Is there anything you can do to make it *more* realistic?

External Reflection and Discussion

1. What are the goals of you and/or your team's gratitude practice? How will you know when you've achieved them?

2. Thinking back to a high-performing team you've been on in the past, how were gratitude and appreciation exhibited?

3. What additional values, changes, and trainings would most support a team culture of gratitude?

10 Gratitude Challenges

*The ability to observe without evaluation is the
highest form of intelligence.*

Jiddu Krishnamurti

I was fresh out of college as a software engineer and had gotten a job in a Speech Technology Research and Development division of a large hardware company. While there, I worked on a short-term project involving text-to-speech technology for Stevie Wonder. Yes, that Stevie Wonder. The popular Grammy winning musician who is blind.

With lots of mentoring and a talented team, we delivered a Kurtzweil music synthesizer that talked to him. (I met him when we delivered it. He played for us and we got to hang out!) This was back in the early 1980s, so, at the time it was a big deal.

That same voice technology is also what the late Stephen Hawking, the famous physicist, used as his voice. Therefore, I'm sometimes introduced as the woman who has "worked with two famous Steve's: Stevie Wonder and Steve Hawking. And she's married to a Steve!"

It took me over 30 years to be grateful for that opportunity. Why? For starters, my boss when I first began with the company—who was a great boss, by the way—was replaced by a crude old man (who threw a quarter down the front of my work colleague's shirt).

Plus, the assignment to work on the Stevie Wonder project felt like a punishment. None of the other engineers wanted it because it was an easy project, more of an application then a challenging research and development venture. It also had to be completed and working in time for a local, live network TV presentation, so finishing it required some all-nighters.

At that point in my life, real gratitude (not the polite, socially acceptable kind) was a foreign concept to me and not part of the department's culture. So, when my new boss told me that years down the road I would be grateful and want to thank him for the opportunity he gave me, I didn't believe him. But that crude old man turned out to be right.

Initially I was resistant to believing that I'd be grateful partly because I didn't believe that my new boss had any smarts, other than technical. Besides, he was nothing like me, so how could *he* know that *I* would be grateful?

The truth is: a strong dislike or resistance to a person or idea can prevent us from being grateful. I learned this while working with a coach and, after expressing a physical repulsion and strong dislike for another person I had interacted with, he gave me an exercise to do.

My coach asked me to list all the people I really disliked. There were two. (There used to be lot more, but I had been a coach for a long time and done lots of work already to improve my interactions and frame of mind when working with difficult people.)

Whenever I said their names or thought of these two individuals—one of whom was a public figure and the other who was in my personal life—it generated a physical reaction. I could literally feel it in my gut, my head would shake, or I would clench my fists.

So, my coach told me to write their names down and look at them for a week. "What you resist persists," he'd say, and when you can see what you're resisting, then you can learn and be grateful. Damned if he wasn't correct.

These two people were unfiltered, loudmouth, blurters who were hurtful and caused pain to others because of what they would say. Eventually though, it became crystal clear to me that they were actually reminders for me to speak up and state my thoughts and opinions. The more I resisted taking these actions, the madder I felt towards these two individuals.

Last week I said one of their names in a conversation and I noticed that I no longer have a physical reaction. I even said something positive about the person. I am grateful to my coach for insisting I do this exercise because now these are two more people I can add to my Gratitude Circle Inventory. (I'm still opposed to their poor behaviors, but view them in a different light: they are people and more than their negative behaviors.)

Being in an environment that doesn't support gratitude or positivity makes it harder to be grateful. If you're willing to look hard enough, there is a lesson and a reason to be grateful in everything. Sometimes the lessons and gratitude just don't show up until years later.

Negative people and environments can be difficult and draining, which makes it hard to get and keep a gratitude mindset, but we always have a choice. We can accept it, try to change it, or leave.

Choosing requires courage and sometimes the best answer is to remove yourself from a situation, whether by walking out of the meeting, transferring to another department, or leaving the company.

Employees who feel powerless are more likely to take the last option and leave the organization. As leaders, we have the power to change this by switching the culture to one of gratitude. One way to do this is to overcome some of the biggest challenges to gratitude. Let's go over a few of them now.

Weakness

Cultures that are high on individualism (as opposed to collectivism) are more likely to see gratitude as a weakness. Individualism implies self-sufficiency. Even Thoreau, who wrote *Walden*, a world-revered story based on his experience of going into the woods to live deliberately and suck the marrow out of life, wished to prove self-sufficiently. (Growing up we'd make regular trips to Walden Woods and hear his story and, as tradition dictated, leave a stone at his cabin.)

Perhaps Thoreau did suck the marrow out of life but, in reality, for the two years and two days he spent alone in the woods, he depended on family and friends to supply his basic needs, like food. Despite loving the solitude, he also kept chairs in his small cabin to welcome guests. Thus, he was dependent on others for survival and wanted visitors, even though he is known for his self-sufficiency.

In societies and organizations that value collectivism and collaboration, gratitude has value. It shows support and caring for others. If you are grateful, it means that you appreciate them, that you notice something about them that has some level of importance or meaning to you. But it is also in the sharing of this appreciation that you become vulnerable to not-so-pleasant things, like rejection.

For example, Sean told Janice that he was grateful for how direct she was when discussing an issue because it made it easier for him to understand. By sharing this value with her, he risked that she wouldn't accept the appreciation he offered, maybe because she didn't label herself that way or because she saw directness as offensive. Plus, Janice now has a potential advantage over Sean by knowing something personal about him.

Being vulnerable can be linked to the animal kingdom. When dogs trust someone, they roll on their back, open wide to show their belly, and allow you to rub it. They don't show their belly to someone they don't trust.

The one difference is that dogs don't have egos, but people do, so it is the ego that gets in the way of our being vulnerable. It is the ego that protects us from opening up our bellies and risking vulnerability, hurt, or shame.

One saleswoman and coach researched mating behaviors in animals after realizing that she was getting more men asking her out on dates than were buying her products and services. She wanted to know why.

Across the board, she found that mating behaviors for animals (and humans) include revealing a vulnerable part of their body, like their neck or wrists, to a potential partner. In her case then, there was a fine line between being open and approachable enough to make a sale and sending an unconscious mating request.

In the days that followed, this saleswoman stopped touching her neck and kept her wrists down and covered when speaking to men and she started making more sales and receiving fewer date requests. She also started teaching an adult education class on how to flirt.

When I was single and dating for the first time in my life at age 44, she taught me these techniques at a large conference and had me practice them. I reeled in four men in one hour. (It was a catch and release program!)

When we show our weaknesses, we are vulnerable and open to the potential of being harmed or rejected. Being vulnerable at work by sharing a mistake or error can also be risky. It can create a fear of retribution or retaliation (sometimes a well-founded one), or of developing a reputation for being weak, incompetent, or dependent on others.

The irony is, when a self-aware leader admits his or her weaknesses honestly and appropriately, it's considered a strength. It creates a connection and builds trust because none of us is perfect.

Rob, a customer service group manager who was physically large and at times intimidating, considered himself self-sufficient. Promoted with no people management training, he was winging it. That is, until he found the courage and admitted to his staff that he didn't know how to be a good manager. He asked for their help, which was extremely hard for him to do.

Rob asked his team to tell him when he wasn't supporting them and to let him know if they were confused by his directions. Each team member talked to Rob one on one and then as a group, and he soon learned that the most important thing they wanted from him was more appreciation and acknowledgement.

While Rob didn't agree with all their suggestions, his team respected him more because he listened. This made him more approachable and a better manager, all because he opened up and shared his weakness. Plus, with their feedback, he changed some simple things, making all the difference.

Thanking people doesn't lessen dependence, but rather builds a work-based relationship. Asking for help, sharing our weakness, and being dependent on others is part of working together collaboratively.

Boundaries

Jeanne, a software director, is one of the most grateful people I've ever met. This woman feels heart-pounding, intense gratitude deeply every day and wakes up each morning being grateful.

Before getting out of bed, she says a prayer of thanks for all the wonderful things in her life and asks for guidance to do right and be a better person. In her daily interactions, she always makes sure she appreciates others, that she values their opinions.

Jeanne estimates that she says thank you 50 or more times a day, never taking credit for anyone else's work and helping others shine, giving them credit publicly. She also ends all discussions asking what she can do to help and inquiring as to whether there is anything she is doing that makes their jobs more difficult.

Jeanne warns that one of the challenges to being this positive and grateful is that some people see you as a pushover. As a result, these particular individuals will test you to see what they can get away with.

What helps Jeanne overcome this potential hurdle is setting boundaries and limits. As a result of being clear about her objectives and what she expects others to achieve, she's enjoyed many successes while operating from a place of gratitude. And no one calls her a pushover.

Underappreciated Hidden Talent

Sue is a part-time medical lab worker and, throughout her career as a chemist, researcher, and medical technologist, she had always received excellent reviews. That is, until one week when, without explanation, her supervisor gave her a satisfactory rating in one category, an action which prevented Sue from getting raise.

Now, Sue had been with this lab for two years and hadn't made one mistake, never missed a day of work, always stayed late when asked, and helped fix instruments when needed. So, the raise itself wasn't even the issue, because it was so tiny. It was more that Sue had been giving the lab her best and was not acknowledged or appreciated for the work she had been doing.

That satisfactory rating changed her attitude about the job and the company. She no longer stayed over and took her time completing tasks. For the first time in two years, she also called in sick.

Sue's work was still high quality, but she was no longer engaged. She admits that, if someone had noticed her just once and told her she was doing a good job, her attitude would have likely changed.

It was so frustrating to her (and to everyone who heard her story) that such a little thing would have made all the difference. But she believes that just one authentic appreciative notice per year would have improved her productivity at least threefold.

The sad side of the story, the part that brought tears to her eyes when telling it, is that her boss would never know her true capacity for work.

An extreme example, Sue's story highlights the challenge that exists for leaders with regard to underappreciated hidden talent. Overcoming this issue involves paying attention to whether you've created an environment, processes, and relationships that support your employees and enables them to speak up and ask for what they need, even if what they need is just a little appreciation.

Complaints and Empathy

Gratitude restores what criticism destroys.

Dan Rockwell

My son spent an entire summer working at an international sports apparel company in the returns department, so his days consisted of listening to what were often angry and mean people share both valid and invalid complaints about certain products.

My son did have some leeway in how he handled these complaints and could, up to a certain level, help the callers. Yet, he was frustrated by the way they approached their complaints. "Don't they know I'm a person," he'd say, "and, if you get me mad, I'm less likely to help you, but I'll go out of my way to help someone who is nice?"

I listened to him make that same statement many times that summer. Clearly many people didn't get it. It's such a simple concept though. Start with gratitude and the voice on the other end of the phone might be more willing to help.

Ten years later, this son is the manager of youth hockey for the NHL's Boston Bruins (ironically, this isn't my goalie son). This is a community relations position and his department puts on more than 100 events a year. What has helped him with these events? The lessons he learned that summer about creating grateful positive relationships.

My son says that he gets more work done with less effort because of the positive relationships he has built based on gratitude and reciprocity. He also notes that angry people who demand things sometimes got results, but not in a sustainable way.

Sarah, who was in New York City on business, learned a similar lesson. Arriving at her hotel the evening before a big meeting, she noticed that the lobby was unusually crowded and abuzz with people, all of whom were obviously angry and confronting the sole desk clerk.

This clerk was a petite young woman who could be heard continuously repeating, "We're so sorry. The renovation construction is behind schedule and the room you reserved with a king bed isn't available. The only rooms left are the small rooms with twin beds. If you prefer, you can make a reservation with our sister hotel a few blocks away for the same rate."

People were roaming around the lobby on their cell phones, complaining to anyone who would take the time to listen. Many refused to go to the sister hotel and were simply looking for new reservations that would put them anyplace but there.

When it was Sarah's turn at the front desk, she looked the clerk in the eye and sympathized. "They've left you out here all alone to deal with this?" she said. "I am *so* sorry. I wish I could jump behind the desk and help you. I'll take any room you have, thank you." The clerk, already on the brink of tears, was obviously moved.

A few minutes after Sarah arrived at her room, the phone rang. It was the front desk clerk, who said, "I have a new room key for you. Would you please come to the front desk to pick it up? Don't say anything."

Sarah picked up the room key and the number emblazoned on it told the story. She'd been upgraded to what was likely the only freshly renovated, unoccupied suite in the hotel. A little empathy went a long way, for Sarah and the clerk both.

Self-Important and Negative People

Perpetually ungrateful people exhibit a sense of self-importance, entitlement, or—in the extreme—narcissism, a mental disorder causing people to have an inflated sense of their own importance. They often come across as arrogant and selfish, even though what they crave most is appreciation, admiration, and praise.

These types of people also typically lack empathy for others. When required to acknowledge someone else's success, the conversation quickly comes back to how great *they* are. They view the world from inside themselves first, which is the direct opposite of a gratitude viewpoint.

Ungrateful people sometimes cause problems at work because others don't want to be around them. Their negativity is contagious, which means that all the benefits of gratitude cannot coexist. Whole teams have been known to implode because of negativity.

Ungrateful people feel entitled to the best jobs, best promotions, and highest pay. They are focused only on themselves and problems and complaints, as well as failures and mistakes made by others, always outnumber the positives.

Managing these people effectively requires choosing your language carefully to avoid sounding critical or that you're finding fault.

Instead, the focus must be placed on the outcomes, goals, and solutions so you don't get sucked into their dissecting, reiterating, complaining, and negativity.

Also, set expectations as to what is possible. Because self-important people feel that they are the center of the world, they want their emails, phone calls, and issues answered and/or addressed right away. If this isn't realistic, let them know.

If the person is unavoidable and important to the job, adapt in a way that is authentic and comfortable to you. For instance, some people are comfortable complimenting and feeding these types of people the praise they crave in order to get things done. Others won't or can't do this just for the sake of the job.

One way I found to handle negative, self-important people is through a combination of authentic praise and light humor. For example, if the self-important person is always on time to a meeting, in a light, caring, and joking way, I might say something like, "Congratulations for always being on time to the meetings, John! I wish everybody was on time and I'm congratulating you on this positive behavior because I know how important accolades are to you."

As always, adapt this strategy to your style and situation, so it is authentic to you and your circumstances. However, be cautious because humor can be tricky. Plus, it's not universally accepted nor as funny if a trusting relationship doesn't already exist.

Having negative people in an otherwise positive group could lead to a few potential outcomes. For instance, the negative person may decide to leave on his or her own because the environment doesn't work for them anymore, mainly since they don't get to complain and aren't the center of attention. They may also be let go for poor behaviors and not fitting in the culture or, alternatively, they may adapt and take on a false attitude of positivity and gratitude in an effort to fit in.

The problem with the last option is that people can intuitively and unconsciously detect when someone is being inauthentic. False gratitude will eventually backfire, partly because it's difficult to sustain. Conversely, when gratitude in the environment is authentic, we can only hope that it will be contagious and change them.

Jeanne Caraglia, a senior director of continuing engineering, says, "I believe that if you consistently treat people with gratitude and kindness, people will eventually appreciate and understand that it is the culture, and they will begin to behave in that way. It's [gratitude] never wasted, it will come back."

Exclusive Versus Inclusive

I'm grateful to have a wonderful manager, a talented team, and for my health. However, we often cannot be grateful unless we have some knowledge or firsthand experience of the opposite, of what it is to have a horrible manager, an untalented team, or to be unhealthy.

Gratefulness encourages inclusiveness, acceptance, and appreciation of extreme opposites like love and hate or wonderful and horrible. When we are inclusive, we see the whole range, the spectrum of possibilities for solving the problem, making the decision, or creating the plan.

This requires using the approach of "and," a method that promotes inclusion, which leads to collaboration, which expands possibilities, which leads to innovation. Being able to simultaneously appreciate and respect a person's accomplishments and skills while disliking his or her behavior of not listening to others is an example of using an "and" approach.

Another example is good communication, which is a give and take that requires both listening and talking. Though they are technically opposites because you can't do both at the same time, the *and* comes naturally in "listen and talk." They are integrated, inclusive, and we have spent a lifetime learning how to do them both.

Acting *and* thinking are two additional actions that act as opposites, especially in areas where you may lack experience, typically requiring thought before taking any action. These actions are even more difficult for those who are more linear thinkers, or those who tend to see only right and wrong or only black and white.

Managers, particularly those in the middle of an organization, benefit from using the "and" approach because, with it, you are:

- Flexible *and* firm
- Innovative (try new things) *and* create stability
- Able to see the big picture strategy *and* ensure details are implemented
- Able to instruct others *and* receive instructions about how to proceed
- Able to support the individual *and* the team *and* the organization

Borrowing from the practice of improv, we can also apply the "yes, and" technique to better achieve the goal of inclusion. Improv starts with and builds on the assumption that there is agreement on the basic situation. From there, the dialogue continues back and forth using "yes, and" to add information until there is a natural conclusion or resolution.

Here's an example:

Situation:

I must paint the house and I have a very small paint brush.

Conversation:

Yes, and didn't I buy that for you?

Yes, and you got it at the same store I shop at for groceries.

Yes, and I have a car and can drive us there in 5 minutes.

Yes, and I noticed it's a small car, like a clown car.

Yes, and that's because I'm a clown.

Yes, and clowns use big props.

Yes, and I will go to the store in my clown car and buy a big paint brush.

Result:

They will drive to the store and get a new paint brush.

Notice how the dialogue went on and on until an effective resolution was reached at the end. Now, compare that to the results obtained from a conversation about the same exact situation, but, this time, without using the "yes, and" technique.

Situation:

I must paint the house and I have a very small paint brush.

Conversation:

No, you don't have a small paint brush.

Result:

Shuts down dialogue, conversation done, and no resolution.

How can you use the power of "yes, and" in business-related conversations, thereby promoting your team and the company as a whole? Here's one example to consider:

Situation:

We need to resolve problem A before the product ships.

Conversation:

Yes, and I heard that problem B happens too.

Yes, and problem B will be addressed in the follow-up shipment.

Yes, and we can brainstorm about problem A for this shipment.

Yes, and we can each suggest a solution to problem A.

Yes, and we can make sure we have all the data for problem A.

Yes, and we can start by stating how problem A shows up.

Result:

The focus is solely on problem A and a process is created for resolving it.

Notice that "no" is not used anywhere in this conversation. Rather than saying, "No, problem B will not be considered for this shipment," it was, "*Yes, and* problem B will be addressed in a follow-up shipment," which continues the focus and conversation on problem A.

Inappropriately or Poorly Executed Gratitude

Showing appreciation can sometimes backfire, especially in the business world. Just go to Glassdoor's website and you'll see comments such as:

- "The Best Place to Work Award is human resources propaganda."
- "You have to be the manager's pet to be promoted."
- "Management only cares about their favorites."
- "Management does not appreciate or see the hard work."
- And on and on…

While some companies poorly execute their gratitude, others spend lots of time and money on staff because they care. They truly want to shift the culture to one of engagement and appreciation.

To create this culture of genuine gratitude requires doing simple things, such as establishing a few processes in which anyone can do the recognizing and people are consistently rewarded when they do a good job. Appreciation forms and boxes can be used, and notes of recognition and appreciation may be sent via email.

For many employees, this works and causes them to appreciate the acknowledgment processes. However, the challenge exists in that, sometimes, your intent and goal do not translate appropriately.

For instance, your remote workers may not understand your processes, or maybe they don't understand why they are important because you don't use appreciation awards. Others might feel pressure to give awards even if it doesn't make sense to them, or they see accolades being dispensed unfairly.

Timely appreciation is just as important. If gratitude isn't given when it's due, it's much like saying, "Good boy!" to your dog a week after you told him to sit. He will make no connection whatsoever to what he did that made you give him praise, and he isn't likely to sit the next time you tell him because a reward given too long after an event loses its potential for reinforcement of the positive behavior.

One person at workshop I facilitated told the story of a manager who had no choice but to ask a new mom to work a weekend. The new mom did, and, when the job was complete, the manager gave her a certificate for a day at the spa. *That* is a timely and relevant reward.

The reverse is true, too. Another workshop attendee told how her boss came from a manufacturing background and had no idea how to deal with professionals. Although she and her team were working on a strict deadline, one day the boss announced that he wanted everyone to take the afternoon off. The intention was to reward them for their hard work, but it was taken as an insult because the deadline still had to be met.

When considering how to show gratitude, whether one-on-one or to a large organization, ensure that it is timely, appropriate, and well-executed.

Gratitude Gone Wild: Include Reality

When I first became enamored with the power of coaching, that's all I wanted to do, coach the world. I was also teaching at a university at the time, so, without realizing it, I was slowly incorporating coaching techniques into the classroom.

Rather than just giving students course-required information, I began asking them questions. This was a graduate-level course for international students, so my "new" approach didn't last very long. These students needed specific instruction and content, and a clear structure for learning. Before I realized this though, a showdown began.

It started as an argument between me and a few students who were taking advantage of me and my newfound vulnerability. It ended in me raising my voice (something I don't do often), yelling at them in my most unprofessional mom-voice.

That's when I realized that I had put myself in a position where I needed to create strong boundaries of what was acceptable and provide a structure with clear learning goals. I began to set classroom ground rules that I still use to this day, which include everything from respecting each other to being on time to no cell phones.

Each industry, organization, and team needs and requires different boundaries based on individual risk and business continuity plans. Though, all must take into consideration the reality that not everyone is good. (Telling Darth Vader to be grateful and trusting doesn't work; you pretty much have to plan for him to be evil.)

Additionally, one singular approach won't work for every situation. It's all about adapting and finding the right balance, which means that gratitude plans must address harsh realities. Creating and enforcing clear ground rules, boundaries, and outcomes helps.

Open the door for gratitude, model it, and act it out. Don't just tell them to practice gratitude because telling alone rarely works.

Avoiding reality also rarely works. Undoubtedly, it will catch up to you in some form.

Takeaways

Gratitude comes with many challenges. Simply telling someone to be grateful doesn't work and changing a culture to one of gratitude in an effort to replace an environment dominated by negative, self-important people is an uphill battle.

Often, gratitude is seen as a sign of weakness and an opportunity to take advantage of a situation. Thus, learning to tailor strategies for each environment and individual by setting clear boundaries and injecting reality are both strategies to consider.

Coming from a place of gratitude and being vulnerable may work in one situation, but not in another. Because gratitude is a comparison of opposites (a nonjudgmental one), what we appreciate is learned from what we do not appreciate.

When we see all possibilities, we look at problems differently. This results in more options, solutions, and choices.

Other key takeaways from this chapter include:

- The transformation to gratitude comes through experience and strengthening the gratitude muscle.

- People who complain and demand might achieve a short-term gain, while those who come from a place of gratitude have longer, more sustained successes.

- Rewards and other expressions of gratitude must be timely and appropriately executed or people may see them as inauthentic and still feel underappreciated.

- The improv technique of "yes, and" supports connection and inclusiveness that leads to gratitude.

Internal Reflection and Discussion

1. Has anyone ever told you to be grateful for something? What was your reaction? Have *you* ever told someone to be grateful? What was his or her reaction?

2. Which of the gratitude challenges are hardest to see in yourself? How might you shine a light on them?

3. Knowing what your gratitude challenges will be, how might you overcome them? Who else could have similar challenges, and how did they overcome them?

External Reflection and Discussion

1. Give examples of each challenge in your environment (weakness, boundaries, underappreciated, etc.).

2. What additional challenges are present in your environment?

3. Discuss the gratitude challenges as a group and list them in the order from the hardest to the least challenging. Include these challenges and possible solutions as part of your gratitude planning.

11

Practices to Strengthen Gratitude

Everything should be made as simple as possible, but not simpler.

Albert Einstein

Hiring people who value and practice gratitude can create a stronger culture of gratitude, but, on its own, this isn't enough. Establishing a culture of gratitude also requires that you align people, technology, and processes from the top down.

Though creating gratitude from the bottom up is important too, work culture starts at the top with senior leadership. It requires constant support by way of actions, behaviors, policies, processes, and more. Gratitude becomes the cultural lubricant that makes all other positive interactions and innovation happen.

There is no such thing as a perfect organizational culture. People *will* resist changes. It's basic human nature. However, continual improvements help maintain and move an organization forward in building a culture of gratitude. Even if that gratitude is not at the forefront, it can still be present, freely flowing underneath.

The more people who practice gratitude within an organization, the more contagious it becomes. The reverse is true too. The more negative the work environment, the more that will spread as well. It is the striving and adapting, the inserting and aligning, that keeps gratitude in the forefront.

Kronos is a company that offers workforce management solutions and it calls its employees "Kronites." If you go to its website, you'll see that it gives a little peek about how it views its staff:

We strive to create an environment that is conducive to the spirit of inspiration and innovation we hold so dear. New challenges can be found behind every door. Not just to advance your career, but to share ideas and explore innovative ways to make those ideas come to life.

Well, Kronos recently moved into a refurbished high-tech tower building in Lowell, Massachusetts that was originally built by Wang Inc., a high-tech company that no longer exists despite making $3 billion dollars revenue per year in the 80s, when it was at its peak.

Inside the towers, the style is similar to what you see with the West Coast tech giants, industrial art deco that has all the bells and whistles: a game room, gelato and coffee bars, hanging chairs, massage tables, and more.

Kronos' website content and employee-friendly structure both scream appreciation for its employees, but it's also what's inside that make its staff happy. It is the people they employ and the processes they put in place that keeps staff coming to work each day. You can see it in the reviews the employees write on Glassdoor, but this company also regularly wins the "best place to work in Massachusetts" award.

Some of the stories you've read in this book are those of Kronites. I've seen firsthand their mistakes, fears, and challenges and know that they are constantly learning and changing while still being productive and profitable. The employees I work with are engaged and dealing with the changes. They're also doing their best to overcome any pockets of negativity.

For example, one employee told me that over the course of six years he's had 22 managers, yet he's still engaged and committed to excellence. Another has shared that she is motivated by the words of the CEO, Aron Ain, which are etched in glass as you enter a conference room on the reception level:

> *Our amazing employees are without a doubt our single most important strategic differentiator, and they make me proud to work here every day.*

This employee, who is also a manager, struggles through the changes and is inspired by the CEO every day. This is critical because we know from research that engagement is a key measurement when effectively managing people.

Kronos also regularly offers a number of different companywide recognition and reward programs. They don't always work as planned when first implemented, but they quickly adapt and change. In this company, gratitude is practiced from the top down *and* bottom up.

Some of the managers are skeptical and game the reward systems for their gain. Others expound on their silliness (or worse). As a company, Kronos clearly sees reality and makes some hard and difficult decisions, as I can attest after having a front row seat to a few of them. However, if an individual or team is committed to growth, positivity, inspiration, innovation, and positivity, creating a culture of gratitude can make all of these happen.

Gratitude is best served when it shows up in the company's vision statements, goals, and strategies. It then becomes institutionalized and can be seen inside and out by being incorporated into processes like performance reviews, rewards systems, training programs, customer relationships, and sales.

When incorporating gratitude, we must also remember that we all give and receive gratitude differently. Educational studies show there are three learning styles:

1. *Visual.* Looking at a beautiful landscape, artwork, a gift, or a picture that evokes gratitude

2. *Audio.* Listening to music, lyrics, a voice, or sounds that evoke gratitude, like waves or the sound of the wind

3. *Kinesthetic.* Dancing, walking, or any other movement that evokes gratitude; touching that evokes gratitude, like touching another person, a soft furry animal, or a smooth edge

Most people have multiple learning styles with one, strong primary focus. For instance, my husband's primary learning style is auditory, so he remembers life events by associated songs or sounds and can only recall our neighbor's names when he assigns a musician's name to them. (We live next to Hank Williams and Sandra Dee, and on the other side is Janis Joplin and Rick Springfield.)

One corporation incorporated all three learning styles to promote a culture shift. It created a beautiful, colorful graphic (visual), printed it on a large, high-quality postcard (kinesthetic), and it offers appreciation stations with a card and box (kinesthetic), both of which are set up in a visually pleasing way at key hallways (visual). When awards are due, they are verbally given (audio) to employees and a physical token is handed out (kinesthetic).

What are some ways that you can institute gratitude into your life and company culture, hitting on all three of these learning styles so everyone in your life feels your appreciation?

Leadership Gratitude Ideas for Your Practice

Fix your eyes forward on what you can do,
not back on what you cannot change.

Tom Clancy

Here are 12 things you can do to express gratitude in a personal way, thereby developing your leadership skills:

Write It	See It	Touch It	Game It
Watch It	Listen to It	Read It	Move to It
Meditate	Volunteer	Do Without	Socialize It

Write it. Every morning, night, or both, list 10 things you are grateful for. Alternatively, write in greater detail 3 things you are grateful for and why.

A variation on this is the gratitude box. With a gratitude box, you take any type of paper you have around—cards, shopping lists, receipts, newspapers—and write in detail one thing you are grateful for, then dropping it into a box (you can also use a jar or similar container). When needed, pull one out and read it.

Once a week, go deeper into what you are grateful about and, also once a week, send a note to a person you are grateful for. Days I don't have time to write, I at least speak out loud as I commute (or to myself if on public transportation; I don't want to scare anyone).

You can also try my *52 Weeks of Gratitude*, which is available online, if you want more help with your writings.

See it. Find pictures that bring you a sense of calm and peace and place them where you can see them often. I use Pinterest a lot for this and have a board of posts that quickly move me to a place of gratitude.

Another option is to create an office space or spend time in a place that moves you to gratitude. I keep lots of pictures, quotes, and a shadow box in mine because they all make me smile.

Touch it. Stand on your feet, feel a breeze in the air, or cuddle with a soft, furry animal. Figure out what types of items create feelings of gratitude in you and keep them close by.

Some examples of items my clients use for this include: a wooden pen, a piece of jewelry, and a rock. One client even finds gratitude in a sleek, silver melon baller.

It doesn't matter what the item is or whether it even makes sense to others. All that matters is that it brings about gratitude in you.

Game it. Each day, count the number of times you say or write "thank you" or otherwise show appreciation. Can you beat yesterday's number? (Also note how often others express gratitude or say thank you to *you*.)

How many people are you grateful for? Do they know it? Have you told them?

Take the People Challenge: For each person you interact with, always verbalize one thing about them that you are grateful for.

For bonus points, do the same for people you despise, dislike, or find repulsive. What are you grateful for about them?

Watch it. Watch a movie, TV show, or documentary. Go on YouTube and watch Brené Brown, TED talks, and other videos that embody gratitude.

Some movies my Facebook friends say make them feel grateful include:

- *It's a Wonderful Life*
- *Blindside*
- *Slumdog Millionaire*
- *Good Will Hunting*
- *Pay It Forward*
- *The Untouchables*
- *A League of Their Own*
- *Harold and Maude*
- *Forest Gump*

Listen to it. What songs make you feel grateful? I have a whole playlist of them. I call it *Whot, Whot!* and every time I hear it, I smile.

Here are a few of the songs my Facebook friends say make them feel grateful:

- "Celebration" (Kool & The Gang)
- "What a Wonderful World" (Louie Armstrong)
- "I Feel Good" (James Brown)
- "Good Vibrations" (Beach Boys)
- "Don't Worry, Be Happy" (Bobby McFerrin)

Read It. Pick up a fiction or nonfiction book, or read blogs, poems, and lyrics that inspire your gratitude. If you have a more analytical side, read about research on gratitude.

Biographies are another option as well. Though I find *Night* by Elie Wiesel hard to read, it always makes me feel grateful. There is also the *Chicken Soup* series, of which there are currently over 250 titles (you can find them at www.chickensoup.com).

A lessor known book you may like and one that is often compared to the *Chicken Soup* books is *Epiphany: True Stories of Sudden Insight to Inspire, Encourage, and Transform* by Elise Ballard.

Move to it. Dance, walk, or run. Take a stroll in nature, or walk a "Grace Trail," a concept explained in Anne Jolles' book, *Grace Trail: Find Your Footing and Move Toward the Life You Were Meant to Live*, where she shares that Grace stands for:

> **G**—What am I Grateful for?
>
> **R**—What do I need to Release?
>
> **A**—What is calling out for Acceptance?
>
> **C**—What is my next Challenge?
>
> **E**—What can I Embrace as possible?

As you walk, use Jolles' questions to ask yourself about grace.

Meditate. You can do this by yourself or, if you're unsure how to do it or need a little help, you may want to try guided meditations.

I use a free app called Insight Timer and my friend John likes the app Gratitude Mediation by Cathy McDonald. Do a search for "gratitude apps" and you will find plenty of options.

Additionally, one of my favorites mediations is "Healing Lake Meditation" by Jon Zabbat-Zinn. You can find it on YouTube or SoundCloud.

Volunteer. Donate your time for something you believe in or to help those less fortunate than yourself.

My first experience with volunteering was in high school, when I answered phones for two years with a drug and suicide hotline.

It was life enriching, educational, and made me so grateful for things I had taken for granted, like food, shelter, education, and family.

Do without. Stop using something that makes your life easier.

For instance, if you normally drive a car, take public transportation instead. Or give yourself a weekly food budget that is half what you'd typically spend.

Doing without makes you more grateful for these types of things.

Socialize it. Create a Facebook game with friends to list 10 things you are all grateful for. Or, instead of a book group, create a grateful group.

Make it a new tradition where, every time you meet with a friend or family member, or before you eat a meal, you say what you are grateful for.

Track your daily practice using the Personal Gratitude Assessment Worksheet or create your own daily gratitude tracker.

Gratitude Practice Ideas for Teams

Here are 12 additional ways to express gratitude in your place of business if your goal is to develop your team's gratitude skills:

Teach It	Verbal Appreciation	Written Appreciation	Gift It
Program It	Daily Huddle	Silent Moment	Game It
Performance	Publicly State It	Core Value It	Culture It

Teach It. Teach gratitude. Offer workshops or trainings in gratitude-supporting skills, such as facilitation, communication, and so on.

Verbal Appreciation. Train managers how to show appreciation appropriately for both individuals and teams. Encourage them to give gratitude in a regular, consistent, and fair way.

Written Appreciation. Show appreciation in emails and/or other forms of communication. A handwritten thank-you note also goes a long way.

A graphic designer who was attending a workshop on gratitude told us that she was working with a client on a newsletter and there was a lot of back and forth.

The client was giving her lots of nitpicky changes and, over time, the emails got shorter and shorter. Some were only one word.

Realizing they sounded abrupt, in her next email, the designer wrote, "I really appreciate you taking the time and caring about the little details in this."

The client was so gushy in her response that the designer instantly saw what a huge difference her simple acknowledgment made. And she realized that her client might have left if she'd continued writing so tersely.

One little change can have a major impact.

Gift It. Celebrate significant events and achievements by giving team members a gift.

For instance, some organizations give one-time gifts to show appreciation to those who go above and beyond. Others regularly hand out gift cards.

Another common way to show appreciation is giving tickets to a sporting event, the theater, or a concert.

Jeanne says that it made her day when the engineering vice president handed her early season Red Sox tickets and said, "I thought you might want to reward someone on your team."

She was extremely thankful that the vice president had given her the tickets to give away and said that giving them to a team member was better than going to the game herself (though her husband disagreed).

Program it. Create an appreciation program or committee and make it accountable to the highest level of management.

Daily huddle. Do a daily team huddle (like Dr. Mary does) and ask: "What are we grateful for?"

Silent moment. In meetings, start or end with a minute of silence, instructing the team to use this time to think about what they are grateful for.

Game it. Make a game out of gratitude by keeping track of who shows it the most.

Louise had a team of 40 people and, when someone went above and beyond what the job required, they got a golden paperclip. Anyone could give anyone else one of these coveted clips (and sometimes they just magically appeared!).

The paperclips added up and, as the year progressed, they could turn them in to Louise in exchange for something.

It was fun, a surprise, and a topic of lots of conversations. Louise loved the role of giving rewards and it created a strong team culture, one that encouraged appreciation of each other.

Review it. Include appreciation and gratitude as a regular part of employee performance reviews. Be clear as to what skills and behaviors are desirable and encourage and support them.

Publicly state it. Include gratitude in reports, status updates, social media posts, and any other way you can to give external kudos.

Core value it. Make gratitude a core value of the organization or team. Have discussions about how to turn it into action with programs and business processes.

For example, at the start or conclusion of a meeting, ask, "What are you grateful for?" or "What went well?"

Culture it. Create a culture where ingratitude is unacceptable and gratitude the norm. This doesn't have to be complicated or cost lots of money either. In fact, getting creative can be crazy fun.

For example, Eric led a team of highly specialized engineers in the semiconductor industry. One day, he asked them to bring in a sturdy bag the size of a grocery sack without telling them what it was for.

A friend of his worked at a well-known, local brewery, so he'd gotten his hands on a few interesting and unique beers.

He found a lab table, lined them all up, and surprised his team by inviting them in.

Each team member could pick out the ones he or she wanted and take a six-pack home. It didn't cost a lot, but it meant a lot to his team.

If All Else Fails Try This

Let us rise up and be thankful, for if we didn't learn a lot today, at least we learned a little, and if we didn't learn a little, at least we didn't get sick, and if we got sick, at least we didn't die; so, let us all be thankful.

Buddha

There will always be moments (or days or weeks) when gratitude is more difficult. Times when the best you can do is struggle to survive, when all you really want to do is give up. Times when you question everything: your beliefs, your faith, yourself. What do you do when that happens?

That is when you want to ramp up your gratitude practice. In business, it's the time to step back and look up. Look up and beyond your personal circumstances. Look at the bigger picture, the strategy, the vision, the sky.

In cases like these, master coach Rick Tamlyn says that there is power in believing that life itself is one big game. That it is all made up. He says that we can and should create the lives we want by continuously playing bigger games.

Bigger Game is even the name of Tamlyn's trademarked processes. He explains:

Instead of waiting for the future to come, why not make up your life as you go? We do this whether we realize it or not. We create mental pictures of our lives. Sometimes they are good, sometimes they're bad, but they're always 'all made up.' These mental pictures are the basis of our created experiences. Remember, your life goes in the direction of the thoughts you carry in your mind and the words that fall out of your mouth.

The Bigger Game is not only for individuals. I've been to several of his workshops and conferences and he invites successful people who've created multimillion-dollar businesses.

Tamlyn says, "If life is a game and it is all made up, why not play a game of your own design—one that excites you, challenges you, and allows you to fully express your talents and creativity?"

I ask, why not make it one that is full of gratitude? It costs very little (if anything), and the return is huge because it *will* improve your bottom line.

Gratitude is sustainable and it is also contagious. As my son says, "I get more done by doing less work because of the positive and grateful relationships established." Or as Jeanne says, "It's [gratitude] never wasted, it will come back." Or as award-winning success author Jack Canfield says, "Gratitude is the single most important ingredient to living a successful and full life."

It's not about getting it right or perfect. It is about starting, right now. Right now, you are not six feet under and that is something to be grateful about. Be courageous. Choose gratitude.

Afterword

By now, I hope you know what gratitude is and the power it offers personally, for leaders, and in its impact on organizations and the world.

Be skeptical, don't believe what I say. Find your own truth about gratitude. Experience it in its fullest.

My wish is that I've given you enough tools and stories that you are inspired and ready to build and strengthen your gratitude muscle, as well as the muscle of your teams.

I invite you to adapt the tools and tips in this book as needed. Establish your baseline using the Gratitude Assessment and then work through the Plan templates. Soon you will see how far you can go, all the way to becoming a gratitude expert.

Most importantly, start now. Develop a simple and easy gratitude process so you stay motivated and regularly practice, constantly building your gratitude muscle.

Change is the only thing guaranteed going forward. Businesses desperately need you as a leader who can drive this change in a positive way to create healthy and positive outcomes.

With every new possibility, opportunities will exist to abuse and misuse change. Be firm, take a stand, and immerse yourself in making change positive.

Cisco, a manufacturer of Internet equipment, projects that, by 2025, everyone in the world will be connected. This connectivity will force the convergence of business, social, physical, and psychological factors, and it will have global implications.

Diversity will become more possible than we've ever seen before and language barriers will become obsolete. Technology and application adaptation will spread like wildfire, upending national and international barriers, policies, and infrastructures.

Humans from all over the world will become more real to each other, more integrated. They'll also become more transparent.

What will a positive future (versus a negative one) be like for you and your team 5, 10, or 25 years from now? Gratitude as an underlying foundation will shift outcomes to positive, and it's something you can start strengthening today.

Maybe you've heard that corporations need to be about more than profit alone. Perhaps you've felt that your business or industry should demand and stand for something, like fair labor practices or sustainable manufacturing.

Do you believe that a positive future like the one portrayed in *Star Trek* is possible? It *is*, but only when built on a foundation of gratitude.

Today, we can see the impact of negativity, especially in social media. In some cases, we have become more polarized, opening the door for fear and hate while simultaneously preventing connection and understanding. As a leader, you can be the one to break through the negative and drive changes that will keep interactions positive and ethical.

Gratitude allows you to engage individuals within the business community. It speeds the change in a positive way, while also dealing with difficult realities. New possibilities are opened up by solving problems in creative and innovative ways.

There will be dark days when it won't be easy to be grateful. These are the times that, the stronger you and your team's gratitude muscle is, the easier it will be to cope.

In easier times, a solid gratitude practice makes things, well, easier. In difficult times, it becomes the lubrication to transformation.

Gratitude is the fertilizer for fulfilling, positive, and meaningful personal and professional lives. It takes the chaotic, stressful, and overwhelming aspects of business and puts them into context so we can smile and lean in with creativity and possibility.

Using your newfound tools and skills of gratitude can be transformational for you and your teams. You now hold the key to turning the tide for your organization, making it healthier, more positive, and more productive.

Having conversations about gratitude seems to spark something in people. Their stories validate its power.

I'm humbled and honored by the overwhelming responses and stories that people have shared about gratitude in both their personal and professional capacities.

So, my only question left is: What is *your* gratitude story?

Acknowledgments

This book shares my lifelong journey of gratitude, a journey that has been years in the making. I appreciate everyone who has helped me get out of my own way and allowed the birth of it. There are so many.

For all the coaches I've had, both past and present. During the process of writing this book alone, I had three! My fellow book-writer and accountability coach, Jennifer O'Keefe, and my spiritual and self-care coaches, Gabriele Ganswindt and Patricia Woods.

To NSA-NE and Stephen Shapiro, who kicked me in the butt to get this book out. To my NSA Mastermind group—Susan Hobbs, Susan Fitzell, Jennifer Howard Elder, and Ingrid Dinter—who picked and prodded me to higher levels.

To Synergy Partners, a Business Networking Group for validating that gratitude in business is a real thing. Once a year they do a tear-jerking "I am so grateful to be alive" gratitude meeting. It was also through them that I met Allison Sica of www.kisstheb-ridewedding.com, the one who did my first ever author photo.

To my friends and board of Star Leadership, past and present, who always listened to my hairbrained ideas, especially Carole Greenfield and Cindy Takvorian.

To my Massachusetts coaches who heard me whine forever about a book: Jane Kalagher, Trish Pratt, Terry Malam Wilson, and Clare Harlow. To the NH coaches connecting group who took this job over from the Massachusetts coaches.

To all the early readers and reviewers, and, in particular, John Ela, who's 245 insightful comments added to the depth of this book.

To Claudia Gere, the expert on all things book-related, who I could not have done without. I learned so much from her. She guided the process in a firm and gentle way and made it real.

To Christina DeBusk an extraordinary editor, she made me sound great in writing!

For the hundreds of clients who've allowed me into their lives at a deep level. Their universally themed stories are shared in a composite way in this book.

To the Coaches Training Institute for teaching me how to be a coach, and to the hundreds more who shaped this book: my mentors, authors, friends, book reviewers, webinar attendees, and many more.

For the petri dish I call my family, old and new, immediate and extended. The Dargin clan is always in my heart.

To my newer family, the Cabrals, for always make things interesting and fun. My family of origin who indoctrinated me the best they could in gratitude.

To my two sons, Mike and Kevin Dargin, who I am so grateful for and proud of the good, caring men they are.

Finally, to my new husband and old boyfriend, Stephen Cabral. I am so grateful for his constant love, support, and encouragement. It wasn't always pretty (me giving birth to this book), but he hung in there and helped me simply by being there.

To you, the reader. Thank you. I truly, from the bottom of my heart appreciate your insights, input, and time.

My wish is gratitude for all.

Love, Star

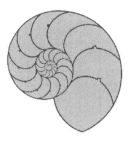

PART 5
APPENDICES

Helpful Resources, Books, and Author's Comments

Gratitude

Simple Abundance: A Daybook of Comfort and Joy by Sarah Ban Breathnach. This is the book that started it all for me. I read it daily and followed her suggestions for almost four years.

Thanks! How Practicing Gratitude Can Make You Happier by Robert A. Emmons, PhD. Love this book! It combines research, history, stories, and reflections on personal gratitude.

Thank & Grow Rich: A 30-Day Experiment in Shameless Gratitude and Unabashed Joy by Pam Grout. I like this book for the author's fun and culturally current writing style (even if you don't follow the 30-day program).

Gratitude: A Way of Life by Louise L. Hay. A collection of essays by almost 50 of the leading gratitude gurus. Read a few a day. Some will resonate more than others.

Gratitude: An Intellectual History by Peter J. Leithart. Does an excellent job of exploring history and the changing shape of gratitude over the years. An expensive textbook that is not for the faint of heart.

Gratitude by Oliver Sacks. A short, life-inspiring book that contains four essays Sacks wrote in his later years.

Grace Trail: Find Your Footing and Move Toward the Life You Were Meant to Live by Anne Barry Jolles. Asking yourself these five life-changing questions can help bring you into a state of "Grace," enabling you to create the life that you truly want to live.

Managing for Happiness: Games, Tools, and Practices to Motivate Any Team by Jurgen Appelo. This is a beautiful, colorful book packed with practical ideas and stories of creating joy and happiness at work.

Communication

The Power of Communication: Skills to Build Trust, Inspire Loyalty, and Lead Effectively by Helio Fred Garcia. Powerful and interesting book using current culture to make points.

Taking Flight!: Master the DISC Styles to Transform Your Career, Your Relationships...Your Life by Merrick Rosenberg and Daniel Silvert. This book uses a fable to explain DISC. The second half is a how to.

Conversational Intelligence: How Great Leaders Build Trust and Get Extraordinary Results by Judith E. Glaser. Brilliant and perfectly maps how to move conversations out of survival lockdown.

Fixing Feedback by Georgia Murch. Feedback, accountability, and leadership topics are all tackled in a straightforward way in this book.

Coaching

International Coach Federation, a nonprofit, global professional organization for coaches. It offers coach certifications, schools, and trainings. You can learn more at www.CoachFederation.org.

Co-active Coaching: New Skills for Coaching People Toward Success in Work and Life by Laura Whitworth, Karen and Henry Kimsey-House, and Phillip Sandahl. Classic coaching book that is the basis for The Coaches Training Institute. You can learn more at www.coactive.com.

What Got You Here Won't Get You There by Marshall Goldsmith. Executive coach Goldsmith talks about common challenges managers face when moving up the chain.

Leadership

Leadership and the One Minute Manager by Ken Blanchard. A classic that is a quick read (and quick to do).

The Leadership Challenge by James M. Kouzes and Barry Z. Posner. Extensive book on all things leadership.

Discover Your True North: Becoming an Authentic Leader by Bill George. A more personal approach to leadership.

Leadership from the Inside Out: Becoming a Leader for Life by Kevin Cashman

"What Makes a Leader?" a *Harvard Business Review* article by Daniel Goldman

"What Leaders Really Do," a *Harvard Business Review* article by John Kotter

Teams and Trust

The Speed of Trust: The One Thing That Changes Everything by Stephen M.R. Covey

The Five Dysfunctions of a Team: A Leadership Fable by Patrick Lencioni

Personal and Business Success

Outliers: The Story of Success by Malcolm Gladwell

Triggers: Creating Behavior That Lasts—Becoming the Person You Want to Be by Marshall Goldsmith

Kiss, Bow, or Shake Hands: The Bestselling Guide to Doing Business in More than 60 Countries by Terri Morrison and Wayne A. Conaway

Winning the Brain Game: Fixing the 7 Fatal Flaws of Thinking by Mathew E. May

Better Than Before: What I Learned About Making and Breaking Habits—to Sleep More, Quit Sugar, Procrastinate Less, and Generally Build a Happier Life by Gretchen Rubin

Rising Strong: How the Ability to Reset Transforms the Way We Live, Love, Parent, and Lead by Brené Brown

Daring Greatly: How the Courage to be Vulnerable Transforms the Way We Live, Love, Parent and Lead by Brené Brown

"How to Become Great at Just About Anything," a 2016 podcast by Stephen J. Dubner. You can find it at http://freakonomics.com/podcast/peak/.

References by Chapter

Chapter 1: Successful Leaders with Gratitude

"What Oprah Knows for Sure." Oprah.com. Accessed May 23, 2017. http://www.oprah.com/ spirit/oprahs-gratitude-journal-oprah-on-gratitude.

MacFarquhar, L. "The Buddha of the Boardroom." *The New Yorker.* April 22, 2002. https://www.newyorker.com/magazine/2002/04/22/the-buddha-of-the-boardroom.

"Marshall Goldsmith 100 Coaches Bios." Marshalgoldsmith.com. http://www.marshallgoldsmith.com/100-coaches/.

Emmons, R. A. & McCloughan, M.E. *The Psychology of Gratitude.* New York, Oxford University Press, 2004. Pages 266–276.

"Editorial Reviews." Amazon.com: Goldsmith, Marshall. Accessed May 23, 2017. https://www.amazon.com/Leadership-Challenge-Extraordinary-Things-Organizations/dp/0470651725.

Stites, A. "Here's a List of Every Major NFL Record Tom Brady Holds and the Ones He Can Still Break." MSN Sports. October 5, 2018. https://www.msn.com/en-us/sports/nfl/heres-a-list-of-every-major-nfl-record-tom-brady-holds-and-the-ones-he-can-still-break/ar-BBNZdNg.

Kouzes, J. & Posner, B. *The Leadership Challenge: How to Make Extraordinary Things Happen in Organizations.* New York, Wiley, 2012. Page 295.

Kotter, J. P. *John P. Kotter on What Leaders Really Do*. Boston, Harvard Business Review Book, 1999.

Schwartz, T. "Why Appreciation Matters So Much." January 23, 2012. https://hbr.org/2012/01/why-appreciation-matters-so-mu.

Welch, J. "Former GE CEO Jack Welch Says Leaders Have 5 Basic Traits—and Only 2 Can Be Taught." Business Insider. May 15, 2016. http://www.businessinsider.com/former-ge-ceo-jack-welch-says-leaders-have-5-basic-traits-and-only-2-can-be-taught-2016-5.

Welch, J. & Welch, S. "Are Leaders Born or Made? Here's What's Coachable—and What's Definitely Not." LinkedIn. May 2, 2016. https://www.linkedin.com/pulse/leaders-born-made-heres-whats-coachable-definitely-jack-welch?trk=mp-reader-card.

Collins, J. *Good to Great: Why Some Companies Make the Leap and Others Don't*. New York, HarperCollins, 2001. Pages 164–187.

Covey, S. *The 7 Habits of Highly Effective People: Powerful Lessons in Personal Change*. New York, Simon & Schuster, 2004.

Covey, S. & Merrill, R. *The Speed of Trust: The One Thing that Changes Everything*. New York, Free Press, 2006.

Lencioni, Patrick M. *The Five Dysfunctions of a Team: A Leadership Fable*. New York, Wiley, 2002.

Winfrey, G. "Four Powerful Things Leaders Should Know about Vulnerability." Inc.com. August 21, 2014. http://www.inc.com/graham-winfrey/brene-brown-on-why-entrepreneurs-should-be-vulnerable.html?cid=search.

Chapter 2: Neuroscience of Gratitude

Cialdini, R. B. *Influence*: *The Psychology of Persuasion*. New York, William Morrow, 1995.

Gallwey, W. T. *The Inner Game of Tennis: The Classic Guide to the Mental Side of Peak Performance, Revised Edition*. New York, Random House, 2010.

Ferriss, T. *The 4-Hour Workweek, Expanded Updated Edition*. New York, Harmony, 2009.

Ferriss, T. *The Tools of Titians*: *The Tactics, Routines, and Habits of Billionaires, Icons, and World-Class Performers*. New York, Houghton Mifflin Harcourt, 2016.

Schwartz, T. "Why Appreciation Matters So Much." Harvard Business Review, 2012.

Losada, M. & Hephy, E. "The Role of Positivity and Connectivity in the Performance of Business Teams: A Nonlinear Dynamic Model." February 2004, The American Behavioral Scientist; Thousand Oaks.

Sugarman, J. "How Many People Does It Take to Build a Bizjet?" *Air & Space Magazine*. August, 2016. http://www.airspacemag.com/flight-today/jobs-bizjet-180959773/#yqoSTLgZ0zEPL5dM.99.

Dizikes, P. "Putting Heads Together." *MIT News*. October 1, 2010. http://news.mit.edu/2010/collective-intel-1001.

Kohn, S. "Let's Try Emotional Correctness." Ted.com. October 2013. https://www.ted.com/talks/sally_kohn_let_s_try_emotional_correctness.

"State of the American Workplace Report, 2017." Gallup. http://www.gallup. com/reports/199961/state-american-workplace-report-2017.aspx ?utm_source=SOAW&utm_campaign=StateofAmericanWorkplace &utm_medium=2013SOAWreport.

Chapter 3: Lessons Lead to Innovation

Potter, E. H. *Pollyanna & Pollyanna Grows Up*. London, Wordsworth Classics, 2012.

Sandburg, S. *Lean In: Women, Work, and the Will to Lead*. New York, Knopf, 2013.

O'Dea, M. "Transcript: Sheryl Sandberg at the University of California at Berkeley 2016 Commencement." Fortune.com. May 14, 2016. http://fortune.com/2016/05/14/sandberg-uc-berkley-transcript/.

Goodell, J. "Bill Gates: The Rolling Stone Interview." Rolling Stone.com. March 13, 2014. http://www.rollingstone.com/culture/news/bill-gates-the-rolling-stone-interview-20140313.

Kerns, C. D. "Gratitude at Work: Counting Your Blessings Will Benefit Yourself and Your Organization." *Graziadio Business Review*. 2006 Volume 9 Issue 4. https://gbr.pepperdine.edu/2010/08/gratitude-at-work/#_edn3.

"The Daily Show—Malala Yousafzai Extended Interview." YouTube: Comedy Central. October 10, 2013. https://www.youtube.com/watch?v=gjGL6YY6oMs.

Chapter 4: Making a Fast Shift to Gratitude

Gladwell, Malcom. *Outliers: The Story of Success.* New York, Little Brown, 2008. Pages 39–42.

"Inside Out." Walt Disney Studios Home Entertainment, 2016.

Chapter 5: Culture and Style Impacts Giving

O'Brien, J. "Giving USA: 2015 Was America's Most-Generous Year Ever." June 13, 2016. https://givingusa.org/giving-usa-2016/.

Heinlein, R. A. *Between Planets.* New York, Ballentine Books, 1951. Page 91.

Bradbury, R. *Dandelion Wine.* New York, William Morrow, 2001. Page 249.

"New Census Bureau Report Analyzes U.S. Population Projections." United States Census Bureau. March 3, 2015. https://www.census.gov/newsroom/press-releases/2015/cb15-tps16.html.

Krogstad, J. M. "Key Facts about How the U.S. Hispanic Population Is Changing." Pew Research Center. September 8, 2016. http://www.pew research.org/fact-tank/2016/09/08/key-facts-about-how-the-u-s-hispanic-population-is-changing/.

"The State of Women-Owned Business Report: A Summary of Important Trends: 1997–2014." American Express OPEN. Accessed May 23, 2017. https://www.nawbo.org/sites/nawbo/files/2014_state_of_women-owned_businesses.pdf.

Aka, R., Barksdale, C., & Hakes, A. "Study of Gender Differences in Expressing Verbal Gratitude." https://www.apa.org/ed/precollege/undergrad/ptacc/verbal-gratitude.pdf.

Morrison, T. and Conaway, W. *Kiss, Bow, or Shake Hands: Sales and Marketing: The Essential Cultural Guide—From Presentations and Promotions to Communicating and Closing.* New York, McGraw-Hill, 2012. Page 256.

"Population Demographics for Lawrence, Massachusetts in 2016 and 2017." SuburbanStats.org. Accessed May 23, 2017. https://suburbanstats.org/population/massachusetts/how-many-people-live-in-lawrence.

Hofstede, G. "National Culture." Geert-hofstede.com. Accessed May 23, 2017. https://geert-hofstede.com/national-culture.html.

Hofstede, G. "What about the USA?" Geert-hofstede.com. Accessed May 23, 2017. https://geert-hofstede.com/united-states.html.

Kashdan, T. B., et al. "Gender Differences in Gratitude: Examining Appraisals, Narratives, the Willingness to Express Emotions, and Changes in Psychological Needs." *Journal of Personality*, June 2009. https://mason.gmu.edu/~tkashdan/publications/gratitude_genderdiff_JP.pdf.

Willyerd, K. "Millennials Want to Be Coached at Work." *Harvard Business Review*. February 27, 2015. https://hbr.org/2015/02/millennials-want-to-be-coached-at-work.

Alper, B. A. "Millennials are less religious than older Americans, but just as spiritual." Pew Research Center. November 23, 2015.

http://www. pewresearch.org/fact-tank/2015/11/23/millennials-are-less-religious-than-older-americans-but-just-as-spiritual/.

Frick, W. "Millennials Are Cynical Do-Gooders." *Harvard Business Review*. May 30, 2014. https://hbr.org/2014/05/millennials-are-cynical-do-gooders.

Marston, W. M. *Emotions of Normal People*. Redditch, UK, Read Books Ltd, 2013.

Langley, T. & Wood, M. *Wonder Woman Psychology: Lassoing the Truth*. New York, Sterling, 2017. Pages 27–40.

"William Mouton Marston: Wonder Woman." Wikipedia.com. Accessed May 23, 2017. https://en.wikipedia.org/wiki/William_Moulton_Marston.

Chapter 6: Mindfulness, Optimism, Happiness, and Trust

Hanh, T. N. & DeAntonis, J. *At Home in the World: Stories and Essential Teachings from a Monk's Life*. Berkley, Parallax Press, 2017. Page 56.

Dalai Lama. *The Art of Happiness*. New York, Riverhead Books, 2009. Page 16.

Goleman, D. & Davidson, R. J. *Altered Traits*. New York, Penguin Random House, 2017. Page 136; Advanced Readers Copy Uncorrected Proof.

Kabat-Zinn, J. Mindfulness-Based Stress Reduction (MBSR) Program. https://www.mindfulnesscds.com/.

Search Inside Yourself Leadership Institute. Google Mindfulness Organization. https://siyli.org/.

Morgan, J. "Is Happiness the New ROI?" *Forbes*. September 12, 2015. https://www.forbes.com/sites/jacobmorgan/2015/09/12/is-happiness-the-new-roi/#3bac5f9d1c26.

Centro.com. Accessed May 23, 2017. https://www.centro.net/careers/manifesto/.

Centro. https://www.glassdoor.com/Overview/Working-at-Centro-EI_IE301536.11,17.htm.

Achor, S. "The Happy Secret to Better Work." Ted.com. May 2011. https://www.ted.com/talks/shawn_achor_the_happy_secret_to_better_work#t-471425.

Rubin, G. "Don't Have to Chase Extraordinary Moments to Find Happiness—It's Right in Front of Me." Forbes.com. July 15, 2011. https://www.forbes.com/sites/gretchenrubin/2011/07/15/i-don't-have-to-chase-extraordinary-moments-to-find-hapiness-its-right-in-front-of-me/#65a055be4351.

Kashdan, T. B. "How Does Gratitude Enhance Trust?" PsychologyToday.com. February 7, 2017. https://www.psychologytoday.com/blog/curious/201702/how-does-gratitude-enhance-trust.

Covey, S. & Merrill, R. *The Speed of Trust: The One Thing That Changes Everything*. New York, Free Press, 2006.

Sharot, T. "The Optimism Bias." Ted.com. May 2012. https://www.ted.com/talks/tali_sharot_the_optimism_bias/transcript?language=en.

Pink, D. H. *Drive: The Surprising Truth About What Motivates Us.* Riverhead Books, 2011.

Collins, J. *Good to Great: Why Some Companies Make the Leap and Others Don't*. New York, HarperCollins, 2001. Pages 84–85.

Goldman, J. G. "Gratitude: Uniquely Human or Shared with Animals?" ScienceBlog.com. December 1, 2010. http://scienceblogs. com/thoughtfulanimal/2010/12/01/gratitude-uniquely-human-or-sh/.

Chapter 7: How to Play the GLAD Game

Wiesel, E. *Night*. New York, Bantam Books, 1982.

"Nobel Acceptance Speech." Elie Wiesel Foundation for Humanity. December 10, 1986. http://www.eliewieselfoundation.org/nobelprizespeech.aspx.

"Oprah Talks to Elie Wiesel" Oprah.com. November 2000. http://www.oprah.com/omagazine/Oprah-Interviews-Elie-Wiesel/2.

Seligson, S. "Elie Wiesel, Spokesman for Peace and Human Rights, Dies at 87." *BU Today*. July 3, 2016. https://www.bu.edu/today/2016/elie-wiesel-obituary/.

"A Guide to the Project Management Body of Knowledge (PMBOK® Guide) - Fifth Edition." Project Management Institute, 2013.

Chapter 8: Assessing Gratitude

Chapter 9: Engage with a Gratitude Plan

Dubner, S. J. "How to Become Great at Just About Anything." Produced by Greg Rosalsky, 2106 Podcast: http://freakonomics. com/podcast/peak/.

Cole, S. "Michael Jordan 'Failure' Commercial HD 1080p." December 8, 2012. https://www.youtube.com/watch?v= JA7G7AV-LT8.

May, M. E. *Winning the Brain Game: Fixing the Seven Fatal Flaws of Thinking.* New York, McGraw-Hill, May 2016.

De Bono, E. *Six Thinking Hats.* New York, Little Brown, 1999.

Shapiro, S. *Best Practices are Stupid: 40 Ways to Out Innovate the Competition.* New York, Penguin, 2011.

Chapter 10: Gratitude Challenges

"Kronos Incorporated Overview." Glassdoor.com. Accessed May 23, 2017. https://www.glassdoor.com/Overview/ Working-at-Kronos-Incorporated-EI_IE2196.11,30.htm.

Stevie Wonder — DECTalk Project. Boston TV. April 29, 1985. http://bostonlocaltv.org/catalog/V_AZC7UMVWLNQGGCX and http://bostonlocaltv.org/catalog/V_IA08EIA3BGTCMDG.

Chapter 11: Practices to Strengthen Gratitude

Tamlyn, R. *Play Your Bigger Game.* New York, Hay House, 2013. Page 94. http://www.biggergame.com/.

Your Next Steps with Star

Gratitude is not fluff, nor is it a cure-all. It does, however, offer huge value and benefits both short and long term to individuals, leaders, teams, and organizations. It can be transformational.

I've made it my life to keep the conversation going and spread gratitude, helping individuals and teams strengthen their gratitude muscle. This has helped them:

- Reduce anxiety and frustration

- Enjoy and learn from the daily work they already do, despite a challenging personal or work environment

- Learn to handle dysfunctional teams or organizations where bad behaviors—like blaming, yelling, and unresolved conflict—are present

- Coach others (whether individuals or teams) so they can move beyond being "stuck"

- Explore more possibilities in problem-solving

- Build personal and team-based customized gratitude practices

- Enhance their leadership style to become more collaborative

- Learn how to use an approach of gratitude to ease difficult or challenging situations

- Learn how to develop positive teams and cultures that engage everyone

- Expose more innovative solutions and risk-taking, leading to bottom-line business improvements

Teams that have a culture of gratitude are more positive, more productive, more engaged, and create more innovative solutions.

Leaders who master gratitude are healthier and able to handle complexity and difficulty with more ease.

For assistance creating, implementing, and managing your personal leadership or team gratitude plan, contact Star Dargin. Browse her website and join her community. Sign up for the newsletter and receive extra gratitude bonuses.

www.starleadership.com
Star@StarLeadership.com

Star Leadership

Key Note Speaker. Come and be inspired. Hear real stories of how gratitude in business have changed individuals, teams, and companies. Leave motivated, with a plan and tons of tips to start or ramp up a gratitude practice. For small groups or groups of thousands.

One- and Two-Day Workshops. Participants complete the gratitude assessment and each person leaves with a personalized plan for themselves and their teams based on their specific business and industry challenges. Lots of interaction with a facilitative approach. Groups of 20 or less are recommended.

Webinars. We frequently offer complimentary one-hour webinars full of practical tips and real-life stories on topics related to leading with gratitude. To receive notices of the dates and times, sign up for our newsletter at www.starleadership.com.

Online Workshop: Confident Leaders from Capable Managers. This six-module workshop leads individuals through the essentials for developing a strong gratitude muscle. It can be taken live or self-paced and includes:

Module One—Defining Gratitude and the Science of Gratitude
Module Two—Gratitude Assessment Baseline and Plan
Module Three—Shifting to Gratitude to Innovate
Module Four—Learn the GLAD Tool, Coaching Teams/Self
Module Five—Engage and Conquer Gratitude Challenges
Module Six—Collaboration, Perfection, and Sustaining

Companion Workbook. The *Companion Workbook* allows you to proceed at your own pace. There's plenty of room for notes and it maps to the book and the Online Self-Paced Workshop, with some additional exercises.

Coaching. Coach with Star or one of her other 20+ trusted and qualified Star Leadership Coaches to build your leadership brand and validate your skills. We work with high-performing, high-potential leaders in companies larger than one-hundred employees, specializing in those who "lead from the middle" (one level below the C-Suite to first-time supervisors). Our customers like us for our consistent and measurable results. They trust us to champion them and their teams.

Consulting. Wouldn't it be great if your employees gushed about what a grateful organization you have, putting you in the top ratings on Glassdoor? It's possible. Each team and organization is unique and one size of gratitude does not fit all. That's why we strategize with you to determine the best way to effectively infuse gratitude into *your* culture.

Follow Star (and FREE Stuff!)

Twitter: @stard111
LinkedIn: https://www.linkedin.com/in/starleadershipllc/
Facebook: https://www.facebook.com/starleadershipllc/
Website: www.starleadership.com

Get extra goodies (like our online gratitude assessment, *52 Weeks of Gratitude* prompts for journaling, a soft copy of gratitude tools, and more!) when you sign up for our newsletter at: www.starleadership.com/newsletter.

To Contact Star

Star@StarLeadership.com

Info@StarLeadership.com (Office Administrator)

Phone: (978) 486-4603

If you liked this book, please write a review on Amazon and share the Gratitude.

Help us bring gratitude to even more organizations!

Order Your Books

Leading with Gratitude: 21ST Century Solutions to Boost Engagement and Innovation

YES! Please send me _____copies. I've enclosed a check for $_____ (made out to Pleasant Vines Publishing) or filled in the credit card information below.

1 book = $14.97

* 10% discount on book orders of ten or more

Shipping & handling is included if you are in the continental United States. Please contact us for shipping rates outside this area.

Please charge my Visa/Mastercard:

Card number: _____

Name as appears on card: _____

Expiration date: _____ 3-digit security code _____

Send my books to:

Name_____

Address 1 _____

Address 2 _____

City _____

State/Zip Code _____

Email your order to info@starleadership.com or mail to: Pleasant Vines Publishing, 185 Pleasant Pond Way, Manchester, NH 03102

About the Author

Star Dargin, PCC, CPCC, has been coaching and teaching since the year 2000. Prior to that, she had an 18-year career in the corporate world, starting as a software engineer, then quickly promoting to Director of Engineering.

As a director, Star managed hundreds of professionals and, at one point, had a bestselling software product that produced more than $500 million in yearly revenue.

Frequently asked about her career change from engineering to coaching, two seemingly different occupations, Star responds that she doesn't feel that they are all that different all and incorporates both in her programs today to "make intangibles tangible"—a process that has ultimately helped her deliver a gratitude-based product that is both measurable *and* achievable.

Star has worked with hundreds of clients and organizations ranging from state and federal governments (NASA and Commonwealth of Massachusetts) to high-tech companies (TEL, Kronos, and many others). She is a highly interactive, nationally recognized presenter and workshop leader specializing in building strong, successful, and grateful leaders who "lead from the middle" of their companies.

Star has developed an inspiring, facilitative approach that helps leaders find the best possible way to identify and tackle challenges, growing in a manner that is both actionable and authentic. She helps them build their brand of leadership with gratitude as the foundation.

Whether delivering a keynote speech or workshop, Star's straightforward, common-sense approach yields positive results. She also loves hearing and connecting with folks whom she has helped make a difference.

Finally, Star is a lifelong learner, reader, and reviewer of books, even though the rest of her family is more heavily invested in sports and music. She actively coaches her two grown sons and calls them her "petri dish." Many of their stories appear in her books and talks.

Made in the USA
Middletown, DE
02 May 2019